Self-e
A Pri
Teach
Guid

Self-evaluation:
A Primary Teacher's Guide

Janet R. Moyles

NFER-NELSON

Published by The NFER-NELSON Publishing Company Ltd.,
Darville House, 2 Oxford Road East,
Windsor, Berkshire SL4 1DF, England.

First published 1988
© *1988, Janet R. Moyles*

Printed by Dotesios Printers Limited, Bradford-on-Avon, Wiltshire

ISBN 0 7005 1180 6

Code 8298 02 1

Contents

Acknowledgements

I acknowledge with gratitude, the contribution of the many primary heads and teachers who gave so much of their time and energy in helping to develop the model, despite all the difficulties of union action, new contracts and curriculum revision. Thanks are also due to the local education authorities involved for the opportunity to use the schools and facilities for distributing draft documents.

A number of other individuals have given valuable support, knowingly and otherwise, among them Ted Ross, Les Bell, Mavis Marvill, Margaret Massie, Alan Beck, Alan Peacock, Sheila Ball and Annie Webster. Many thanks also go to Brian, my husband, who patiently read drafts, corrected proofs and put up with all the general inconvenience caused by writing books and theses.

Finally, acknowledgement must be given to the contribution of my publishers for allowing me the opportunity to share this research with a wider audience of committed people.

Janet R. Moyles

Introduction

As a primary school teacher or as one involved in primary education, you, the reader, must have asked yourself on frequent occasions: 'What have I achieved today? What have I really taught and the children actually learned? What are the most important aspects of my teaching? What are my main strengths and weaknesses? What gives me greatest job satisfaction?' And maybe: 'Why do I find this job so frustrating yet so enjoyable? How can I make a better job of what I do? Where should I be going now in the profession?'

It is quite likely that you have voiced your thoughts to other teaching colleagues and explored various answers and possibilities. You may have discussed your future prospects with the head or been on in-service courses to enhance your professional understanding and performance in the classroom. It is possible that, despite all your efforts, you still need help in making sense of and evaluating your role as a primary school teacher.

This is and should be the basis of teacher appraisal. The Department of Education and Science (DES) document 'Better Schools' (GB. DES, 1985) suggests 'all teachers need help in assessing their own professional performance and in building on their strengths and working on limitations identified'. The starting point must be the teacher herself* embarking, at least initially, on some form of self-evaluation. But how are individuals to know, except intuitively, what it is they are evaluating and does this compare with other primary teachers opportunities for assessment of themselves?

There is an obvious need for a carefully conceived document, applicable right across the primary age range (three- to eleven-year-olds), by which teachers can compare their own personal and individual performances and yet which gives a cohesion to a range of such self-evaluations and a system of agreed principles on which this should operate. Such a document is the subject of this book and an integral part of it (see Appendix C).

The model presented here highlights all the many features identified as constituting 'the effective primary teacher'. It incorporates elements related to both teaching skills and processes and sets them firmly in the context of schools. Its development by a teacher, with teachers, for teachers has proved to be its greatest strength. As a criterion-referenced system it is capable of being used by a wide variety of different teachers within the three to eleven age range in many contexts. Simplicity in use has also proved to be an asset to busy teachers. Rather than sitting on the edge of an uncomfortable system, the model reflects and is a part of everyday classroom life and teachers have felt able to adopt its checklist format as an aide memoire to evaluating their role as primary teachers.

The model's main use, however, is as a self-evaluation document within a system of teacher appraisal. The reasons for the current pressure for systematized teacher appraisal lie within the notion of general accountability and demands for higher standards. The first chapter takes a brief look at the rise in demands for accountability within the education system and the consequent calls for teacher appraisal. Chapter 2 skims through some past and present research into what constitutes effective primary teaching and the consequences of this in attempting to develop any model for self-evaluation. The underlying rationale and principles of the model are given in Chapter 3, with some pointers as to the

---

* Throughout the document the feminine gender is used *only* for ease of expression. Male colleagues can feel themselves well and truly involved!

advantages of this type of self-evaluation. Details on how to use the current model are set out in Chapter 4, which also suggests how the results might be interpreted. Chapter 5 deals with self-evaluation in the whole context of teacher appraisal and outlines ways in which individual teachers might benefit from involving colleagues and others. (Suggestions for activities to pursue with colleagues are contained in Appendix B.) The final section contains some speculative comments as to what is the likely future for teacher appraisal systems. A synopsis of the research from which the document evolved is the subject of Appendix A.

First, then, I turn to the general and current issues regarding teacher appraisal and explore the needs of all parties concerned in primary education. For as Millman (1981) emphasizes '. . . the evaluation of teachers is a serious business, for it goes on in the midst of life and concerns the well-being of people. A process like that is not trivial. It is worth our attention and worth doing well'.

1

The 'roots' of appraisal

With public opinion of teachers at a relatively low level and political pressures high, morale has understandably fallen significantly over the past few years. A *Times Educational Supplement* (TES)/MORI poll just prior to the general election in 1987, reported two-thirds of all teachers to be concerned about low morale in schools. Despite this, most primary school teachers continue to pursue their escalating tasks with good humour and enthusiasm and thus provide a sound education for the children in their care.

It seems that discussions and negotiations on such a contentious educational issue as teacher appraisal, were considered only after the press had reported the whole matter in highly emotive terms. Salaries equated with performance and dismissal for ineffective teachers were but two of the suggestions which set all the alarm bells ringing in teachers' minds. Primary teachers owe it to the conscientious people they are, to tell the nation just what their job entails and how well they do it. They need the opportunity to set down definitive statements to justify their worth. Teachers need evidence as to where their effectiveness is marred or influenced by variables over which they have little control.

Currently, most teachers feel that they are already stretched to the limits in coping with their ever increasing curricular demands without any other 'unnecessary' impositions. Yet assessment, particularly a supported self-assessment of a primary teacher's role, could well aid teachers in their everyday efforts to secure a better education for children. In turn, it is likely to increase job satisfaction and, more importantly, give evidence to the outside world of the depth and complexity of the primary teaching role. Jackson (1979) sees this as no mean feat when he suggests

> Class sessions, like bubbles, tend to be shortlived, and after a teaching session is finished, its residue, like that of a burst bubble, is almost invisible . . . we need to become more aware than we presently are of the fleeting and ephemeral quality of much of the teacher's work (p. 31).

In clarifying expectations and detailing workload, one might reasonably expect heightened morale.

The notion of accountability

Whatever the school or classroom situation, and however it appears, teachers are constantly observed and monitored by various people, colleagues, head teachers, advisers, parents, children – just as they themselves constantly monitor and observe. Teachers have long respected their role in the hierarchy of accountability, exemplified in Figure 1.1. The relationships between the teachers and the other parties to whom they are responsible for the education they provide the children in their care are clear. Whatever system of appraisal is adopted it must satisfy all parties – the government, the new governing bodies, the public, the unions, individual teachers and, most importantly, the children. Whichever schools they find themselves in, children must have similar and equal opportunities to learn at their own pace, in a pleasant and enjoyable environment and be given every possible opportunity for development of their individual talents and potential.

Figure 1.1: The web of accountability

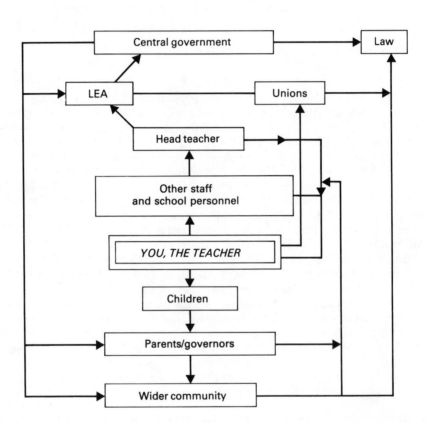

Parents, in all good faith, hand their children over to us and most have high expectations that their children's education will be superior to their own. Governors are elected who, in pursuance of their duties, must safeguard for the community at large the quality of education within their particular institution. It would be equally true to say that teachers owe it to their teaching and non-teaching colleagues to perform in such a way that the reputation of the school is enhanced: otherwise the poor performance of some is reflected in the reputation of many. Additionally, we all have a duty to the local education authority (LEA) and its elected representatives to provide the highest quality education to justify the financial outlay on salaries, buildings and resources. The LEA is in its turn accountable to the electorate and ultimately to the government. After all, when one considers that public expenditure on education amounts to as much as one-fifth of the gross domestic product, this is a reflection of the value attached to a system, the evaluation of which is a relatively difficult issue due to its pragmatic and temporal nature. It goes without saying that this is a heavy burden of responsibility for teachers and one for which it seems they are rarely given credit or acknowledgement despite a majority who work conscientiously and unstintingly at their duties.

Simplistically, of course, accountability reverts ultimately to the individual teacher as a member of society and a tax and ratepayer – as good a reason as any to evaluate what one does! In other words, we owe it to ourselves to be effective in the role of primary teacher.

Perhaps a brief synopsis of the historical and social reasons for the accountability structure is needed in order to give teachers a greater understanding and a whole perspective on the current situation. The main features are now explored.

Accountability in the early days of state education

From the inception of state education and the creation of an Education Department in 1856, political and public demands for accountability have been manifested in such schemes as the 'payment by result' system which attempted to assess teacher's performance in terms of pupil examination results in the three Rs and school attendance. The Cross Commission of 1886, recognized the need for modification and relaxation of this odious situation but stressed the need for greater facilities for the training of teachers in requisite skills. However, it was not until the publication of the Elementary Code in 1904 (the wording of which, incidentally, documents high ideals for teaching and learning at that time which still prevail today) that there was any explicit statement of objectives by which a teacher could be assessed. By this time, education was in the hands of local authorities though monitored by H.M. Inspectorate whose activities are well documented in school log books and whose visits were anticipated by teachers of the time with dread.

From the early part of this century, the traditions of the education service began to reflect the democratic nature of our society and various government legislatures have led, according to Green (1981)

> to such diversity of devolved and delegated power, responsibility and training, that accountability in any formal . . . sense cannot exist. Rigidly defined roles and strict hierarchy with rules and regulations detailing procedures are needed for simple, tight accountability (p. 43).

Though the desirability for this type of process is questionable, some definition of 'good' teaching undoubtedly needs conceptualizing before assessment of teachers' performance is practicable. Little research into the constituents of effective teaching occurred in this country between the wars or immediately after the Second World War, although there was a plethora of such studies in the United States which influenced thinking in Britain. Similarly, the post-war period saw an influx of scientific management procedures and skills from the USA of which accountability in the hierarchy was of vital interest.

The 1950s, 1960s and early 1970s

Psychometric testing methods, already widely employed during the 1950s and 1960s in commercial and industrial assessment procedures, were at this time imported into the field of education, vocational selection and evaluation. The thinking behind this strategy was that little in-service assessment of a teacher's performance was necessary if the person concerned had been adequately vetted before and during training. The inadequacies of such methods were, however, recognized relatively swiftly. This period rapidly developed into a 'boom' time for education, with money being virtually no object and investment in schools and education being on a scale never before or since envisaged. The failure, however, of such vast expenditure to produce any real concrete evidence of improved educational standards and the sudden oil crisis of 1972 with its resultant economic slump, brought a new cry for accountability of the nation's schools and personnel. In addition, the Plowden Report of 1967 had created the requirement for a rethinking of educational needs and objectives and highlighted the desire for quality, efficiency and effectiveness in all areas of primary education, including its resourcing and staffing.

The ideals of the Plowden Report were never totally fulfilled as, by the mid 1970s, primary school rolls were falling, a factor which in itself created yet a new call for educational accountability. This was compounded yet further by the William Tyndale School 'scandal' (Auld, 1976) which drew public and government attention to the need for evaluation of the roles and functions of primary teachers.

Moving towards the present day

James Callaghan's Ruskin Speech of 1976 and the Green Paper of 1977 both focused sharply upon the work of teachers and schools. Since that time education has increasingly been subjected to a scrutiny on a scale never before undertaken. The publication of HMI Reports on individual schools and general educational issues and the advent of assertive and prescriptive curriculum documents, has served to focus political and public attention on educational processes and products. The requirement on schools to produce an individual brochure for parents and others stating aims and objectives has also highlighted public, and in particular parents', awareness.

The emergence of more formal schemes for teacher appraisal can undoubtedly be traced, however, to the development, particularly in secondary schools, of school self-evaluation and curriculum review. Although basically aimed at appraisal of the institution, it was an inevitable development that individuals within schools would equally become the focus (see the documents produced by the Inner London Education Authority (ILEA) in 1977 and by Oxfordshire in 1979). Further political endorsement of this came in March, 1983, with the publication of the White Paper 'Teaching Quality', in which the government advocated the formal assessment of teacher performance. The then Secretary of State for Education stressed the need for formal appraisal of teachers in his speech at Sheffield in 1984, saying

> I believe that every LEA should have accurate information about each of its teachers, vital for career development and that information should involve an assessment of performance based on classroom visiting and appraisal of pupils' work and the teacher's contribution to the life of the school. I welcome the willingness of LEAs and teachers to grapple seriously with these difficult problems.

Hot on its heels followed a number of documents the most recent of which, 'Quality in Schools: Evaluation and Appraisal' (GB. DES, 1985) concludes that teacher appraisal seems 'to bring about some improvement both in teacher's understanding of what is expected of them and in how others see their performance in the classroom and more widely' (p. 43). The core curriculum and national testing of children's competence in the basic skills highlight even further the need for teachers to be aware of their own classroom skills and their effectiveness in promoting children's learning.

This succession of government publications, culminating in the 1986 and 1987 Education Acts and their many implications, have attempted implicitly and explicitly to pursue the question of accountability by increasing the participation of governors and parents in school organization and administration. It is evident that, while constituting something of a threat at present, appraisal at both local and national level is imminent and primary teachers must prepare themselves for the inevitable.

In this climate it makes sense to consider by what means appraisal can occur, who should be involved and what will be the effects of such appraisal, rather than considering whether appraisal should take place. For as Sockett (1982) suggests 'If . . . the profession was able to articulate what it regarded as the positive standards of good teaching, it would itself be providing a measure of accountability' (p. 18).

Accountability and the role of the primary school teacher

As has been indicated, it is quite difficult to define exactly what we are accountable for: the 'products' of primary teaching can only play a little part in its evaluation as the younger the children, the more dilemmas in trying to produce formal outcomes of their learning. Any test, such as those integral within the national curriculum at ages seven and eleven, can demonstrate only a relatively insignificant part of any learning. Yet, as clearly indicated above, we as teachers must be accountable for aspects of our work which interest the various parties already identified.

In truth, many teachers actually welcome the opportunity to promote their work to others: much time and energy has been devoted by them all, whether initially Certificate of Education trained, graduates or post-graduates. There is an eagerness on the part of an increasing number of teachers to pursue their initial qualification into further professional study, yet primary teachers do not always market their skills to best effect. Probably the main reason for this is the subjective nature of the work they do. Much of primary teaching needs to be 'appropriate' to particular and often individual children. Yet what is appropriate to one child does not hold good for others. As HMI assert in 'Primary Schools: Some Aspects of Good Practice' (GB. DES, 1987)

> The high quality of teaching was the strongest feature common to all the examples in this publication. As might be expected there were variations in the teaching styles reflecting the needs of the situation and the personality of individual teachers (p. 33).

There has to be some means of defining and justifying the skills which lead to and stem from this high quality teaching and ultimate learning. Being accountable for what one actually does automatically follows.

So what is it that primary teachers actually *do* in order to facilitate children's learning? What should they assess themselves against? If teachers can define what they feel the job of primary teaching is all about, then others can equally evaluate their relative skills. Yet how does one assess one's impact on children in these formative years of education? Teaching is a very positive job, yet who can assess the character building elements of teaching? Why does one teacher seem better able to promote and sustain learning than another? It would be a very brave soul indeed who tried to answer all these imponderable questions!

Watching primary teachers 'in action' one is rapidly made aware of all the many skills and talents they do use. Listing them is less easy! In 1972, Duthie reported on a remit he had been given by the Scottish Education Authority to make 'an objective analysis . . . of the educational activities on which primary teachers spend their time ' (p. 87). He and his team found themselves 'overwhelmed by the complexity of the situation' and reported little agreement as to what they had really seen! Fifteen or so years later, one feels he might have found the situation even more impossible!

There is obviously a need to explore past and present attempts at identifying the concept of 'effectiveness' in relation to teaching primary children in an attempt to consider the content of the present model. The next chapter explores the notion of teacher effectiveness and the contribution research findings have made to the present model.

2

What is 'effective teaching'?

The epitomy of effective teaching would appear to be the occasions during which what the teacher teaches is what the child learns – and we all know the impossibility of that even if we recognize its merits! But how may we go as far as possible in attempting to achieve this goal?

It is clear that any attempt to produce criteria by which teachers may be assessed is fraught with difficulties. Yet without such written evidence of their role it is impossible to impress on others, particularly parents, governors and the wider community, that is those not directly involved in teaching themselves, the complexities of the primary classroom and interactions with children across the three to eleven age range. Arguably, what happens in classrooms catering for primary age children has often to be viewed in an holistic way rather than as a set of analysable individual components. For example, the child will be using overlapping skills with handwriting when painting and reading. Yet any model of teaching assumes as least some individual elements. Cognitive aspects of learning withstand evaluation, to a certain extent, but much of primary teaching is in the affective domain and defies formal assessment.

Barrow (1984) is rightly concerned that many good things that teachers attempt to do with and for their children are not capable of measurement or descriptive evaluation except 'by arbitrarily reducing "quality" to a set of more or less directly observable behaviours that as likely as not have no bearing on the question' (pp. 253 and 268). He also argues that the freedom of teachers would be improperly limited if they had to see their job in terms of fulfilling behavioural objectives decided by others (p. 176). What it seems is needed is a written indication of a 'vision' of teaching that is above anecdote but which encourages teachers to view their role eclectically and, as importantly, methodically. It must also concentrate on significant features of teaching rather than on the finest details.

If assessment procedures are to be worthwhile to everyone concerned, and not just another burden on limited time and resources, it is vital that we, the primary section of the teaching profession, decide for ourselves just what does indicate areas of 'effective teaching'. Of one thing we can be certain, if we do not do it ourselves we shall soon have methods imposed upon us which may not be to our liking.

Because of the enormous complexities of primary classroom life, and the obvious difficulty for an external evaluator to observe and understand all aspects, any model of effective teaching must be capable of use as a self-evaluation document – at least in the first instance. To be called a true 'model', it must also have an underlying rationale based on current and previous research findings. A brief synopsis of this research will reveal its usefulness in terms of the present model.

Research into effective teaching

In Britain, prior to the publication of the Plowden Report (1967), the question of effective teaching had not occupied a major place in research other than in areas related to teacher training. The implied notion was that teachers, in their initial training, 'absorbed' effectiveness skills and retained them indefinitely! Conversely in the USA research on teacher effectivness has been conducted for nearly 70 years. This existing wave of research at all levels of schooling was escalated during the 1970s with the advancing need for accountability. The idea of 'minimum competencies', according to Nuttall (1982), has become a very important notion in the USA with no fewer than 38 states having them 'enshrined in law' (p. 15). It would appear helpful to look first at the American literature before turning to British studies.

Research in the USA – the early days

According to Dunkin and Biddle (1974), more than 10,000 publications on teacher effectiveness have been identified prior to 1963. Even by American standards, this must represent an awful lot of thinking on the subject. The accumulated literature is so overwhelming that even bibliographies (for example, Domas and Tiedeman, 1950, Morsh and Wilder, 1954, Barr, 1961, and Powell and Beard, 1984) have become unmanageable. Suffice it to say that the history of research into teacher effectiveness reflects a gradual evolution of perceptions of 'effectiveness'. The main bulk of earlier studies considered effective teaching to be related to such things as teachers' personality traits and the particular characteristics possessed by the teacher. The use of rating scales (teachers and pupils), personality measurement, checklists, field notes, questionnaires, theoretically based observations and interviews was a natural consequence of this thinking. American research was also fond of correlational techniques where one factor of teacher effectiveness, that is a measure of personality, was assessed against, for example, pupil attainment on a test. Readers will no doubt baulk at this suggestion particularly at present!

The emphasis on predictive and productive features has been criticized by many writers, for example Kyriacou and Newson (1982). They feel strongly that these early studies did little to advance knowledge of teacher effectiveness, mainly because they dealt insufficiently with the process and context of teaching and learning. Schmid (1961) sees the lack of success resting on the fact that

> Teaching is a complex activity carried on in a complex environment – the school. It is directed by complex organisms – human beings. The recipients of the teaching activity are complex individuals, students, whose characteristics are undergoing continuous and complex change . . . It is difficult to define teaching effectiveness because the elements in effective teaching apparently are not only legion but also are intricately interwoven (p. 23).

Each of these earlier studies, dating from just after the First World War until the late 1960s, is characterized by the researchers' enormous difficulties, particularly in elementary schools, in identifying any real objective measures of teacher effectiveness. Many checklists were devised and refined but the studies have all failed to reach a finite consensus as to what constitutes good, effective teaching.

Many writers have been most critical in their reviews of these earlier studies. However, their usefulness cannot be disputed in terms of the fact that clearly research had to begin somewhere. A lot of ground was covered in identifying measures and methods which were *not* useful in assessing teacher effectiveness! What these studies did was to clarify and highlight the need for systematic observation of specific teacher and pupil behaviours and interactions in the context of the classroom and the school.

Research in the USA – 1960 onwards

This multiplicity of studies, only hinted at above, has gradually moved from research into relatively limited domains of teacher effectiveness to the study of teaching and learning situations. Gage (1963) and Smith (1960) both feel strongly that looking at effective learning is examining a totally different phenomena from effective teaching. They maintain that conceptually the two are independent. Thyne (1963), however, feels that to teach effectively teachers must have insight into the nature of learning and how to make learning take place (pp. 14–15). This point was taken up by Denham and Lieberman in 1980. They go further by suggesting that teachers 'must know the cognitive skills and level of performance of individual students' (p. 24).

Evertson and Brophy (1974) studied teachers of second and third grade elementary pupils. They found that the most highly effective teachers, with all socio-economic levels of children, were those who

1 were organizationally sound;
2 were extremely flexible;
3 were constantly assessing their own and the children's learning;
4 were geared to problem solving techniques for themselves and their pupils;
5 had high expectations;
6 took 'personal responsibility for the learning of their students' (p. 39).

Similar theories were developed by Gagne as early as 1970. He concluded that the most effective teachers were those who gave close attention to individual differences and needs of learners. Flanders (1970) developed an interaction analysis system in an attempt to discover which situations made for effective teaching and learning and pioneered many studies in this area. However, the value of his system lay in its pioneering qualities rather than in any results achieved: it was quickly recognized that classroom interactions are too complex for any one method of study.

McKenna (1981) views evaluation of teacher effectiveness as being based very soundly on materialistic principles. He names 12 which include in-service training (INSET) opportunities, time and number of students, marking conditions, resources, and community characteristics (p. 23). He adds, however,

> evaluation must embrace what teaching and teachers do to make the years spent in schooling . . . as full-living, wholesome, democratic and fulfilling as can be conceived, to a substantial degree independent of cognitive learning outcomes (p. 24).

Doyle (1983) identified 19 'important instructor characteristics' (p. 36) which appear to include all those previously mentioned with variations on the original theme! What is clear is that no one writer *is* clear about what actually constitutes an effective teacher!

Many of the above writers are sceptical about whether teacher effectiveness can ever be successfully defined and, in consequence, evaluated. Others, including Ryans (1972) and Millman (1981), believe that teacher effectiveness *can* be defined and evaluated given certain prevailing conditions.

Despite the apparent contradiction between these groups of writers, there are points which emerge over which they all seem to agree, namely :

1 Evaluation must be linked to improved performance.
2 The effective teacher cannot be judged by correlation with pupil achievement.
3 A teacher's duties and responsibilities must be clearly defined in school and on an individual job description basis and, as some writers suggest, on a teaching profession level, like medicine and law (e.g. Iwaniki, 1981).
4 Teachers must play a part in any evaluation (perhaps through staff appraisal interview situations) but preferably within a whole school evaluation built into the process of assessing individuals.

5 Assessment must be part of an on-going process because of its cyclical nature explained by Figure 2.1.
6 Self-evaluation probably holds the key to the future assessment of teachers.
7 Self-evaluation requires that teachers possess a high degree of confidence in their abilities and, therefore, flexibility. The influence for this is likely to come from initial training, in-service training and, most importantly, their own self-image. This, of course, is influenced by the government's and public's value judgements of teachers.

McNeil (1981) summarizes this last aspect in suggesting that parents and the public want 'the establishment of authority, an authority of values, standards and guiding purpose', while teachers 'want to feel their worth as teachers is unconditional' (p. 279). We can only wholeheartedly agree with this opinion.

Figure 2.1: Cyclical nature of evaluation

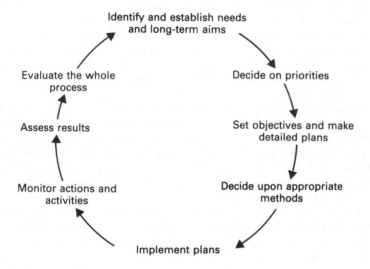

Research in Great Britain

Much of what has been said about American research, content and methods, has been reflected in British studies only from a later period. Among the first major British studies was that conducted by Morrison and McIntyre in 1969. They found that all classroom observation of teacher effectiveness suffered from being unable to take in all the variables of the situation at any one time. It, therefore, did not do justice to the complexity of either tasks or relationships. They saw the greatest difficulties in assessment as undoubtedly lying in 'the areas of social attitudes, moral development, social maturity and personality traits' (p. 20). Morrison and McIntyre even hinted at self-evaluation, saying

improved motivation also depends on teachers being willing to examine their own techniques and principles of instruction in the light of information already available and being prepared to modify their behaviour (p. 150).

The Weaver Report (1970) saw monitoring of standards and enhancement of professionalism as attainable through the formation of a teaching council for all teachers.

Such a council would be responsible for control over entry to the profession and for the discipline of its members. The notion of a teaching council has recently been raised again by teachers' unions, this time in relation to the accountability of the profession, and, by implication, the assessment and monitoring of teacher effectiveness.

Duthie (1972) mentions all the many tasks undertaken by primary school teachers which are non-educational and yet contribute to effectiveness within the classroom. Such factors are even now again under great scrutiny in relation to the teachers' new contract and the negotiation of hours. More difficult to consider in this context is the suggestion by Rosenshine (1979) that flexibility, enthusiasm, energy and animation are major contributory factors to teacher effectiveness. That it is possible to put either an hourage or an assessment on such features must be in question. Yet another difficult area was raised by Nash's research in 1973. Based on a participant observer approach, he found that teacher expectations were highly significant in effective teaching and learning.

A major study of its time was the Ford Project (1973 to 1975) under the leadership of Elliott. Elliott and his team instigated research with a group of teachers into how to monitor and reflect on their own teaching effectiveness. This series of studies was characterized by the fact that subjects were, on the whole, chosen because of their lack of effectiveness in the classroom. By working with them, the team were able to analyse such factors as motivation, threat and the ability to self-evaluate. Elliott and his colleagues found that there was really little opportunity in schools for teachers to undertake any form of self-evaluation, monitoring or reflective teaching. He and his team suggested and practised through meetings, the idea that self-assessment should also involve other teachers, on the principle that 'the more access a teacher has to other teachers' classroom problems, the greater his ability to tolerate losses in self-esteem' (p. 46). Elliott found significant evidence to suggest that 'personal identity was intextricably linked with their [the teachers] professional role in the classroom' (p. 44). In Unit 2 of this study, Elliott and Adelman reaffirm

> Our key concept was that of the consciously self-monitoring teacher. Such a teacher attempts to formulate to himself and others true descriptions and explanations of his conduct. A concern for truth, but not necessarily its achievement, is built into the concept (p. 14).

Many British studies appear to have steered clear of actually itemizing what constitutes an effective teacher and the reader has often to infer the researchers' views on the subject. Squires (1982) rues this fact, wanting something more definitive. He theorizes that teaching has five major dimensions, which have been restated and illustrated in Figure 2.2 (author's own interpretation).

Squires believes strongly that students' performance cannot be used in ratings of teacher effectiveness and that really useful evaluation comes from teachers reflecting not just on the children they teach but, most importantly, on themselves as teachers.

Becher and colleagues (1982) express a clear commitment to self-evaluation in suggesting that other forms of accountability will 'only increase external control over schools without being able to translate that control into improvements in the quality of teaching'. They go further in suggesting 'auditted self-assessment', that is self-assessment audited by an adviser, which would have the advantage of an external professional opinion but based on a teacher's own analysis. Dean (1982) also suggests self-assessment as the best means to becoming more effective teachers but is also of the opinion that teachers should equally be open to assessment by colleagues (p. 152).

Figure 2.2: A model for teaching

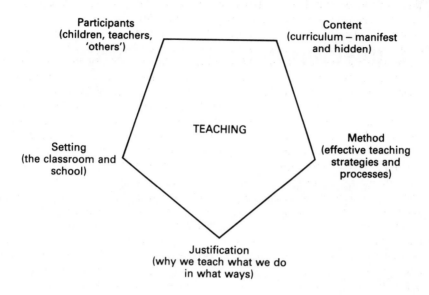

Some conclusions about the research

Despite all the research, British and American, an objective criteria for assessing the effective primary school teacher is still elusive, as is a suitable methodology. Studies appear only to touch the tip of the classroom iceberg. The writer's own view echoes that of Britton (1969) when he suggested 'If a teacher could be more certain what learning looks like, in some of its many guises, he might find it easier to monitor his own teaching' (p. 81). Nevertheless, teacher effectiveness *must* be monitored both in teachers' own interests and those of their pupils and, as we have already seen for the purposes of public accountability. The criteria to be used must be based on many factors other than the purely pedagogic. The methodology must be flexible and easy to operate, preferably in the context of self-evaluation. The content must draw on the many identified skills and characteristics of the effective primary teacher as well as on the processes, context and constraints within which teaching and learning take place. All these identified factors formed the basis of the final model. The next chapter defines the model's rationale, discusses the involvement and thoughts of teachers and describes its advantages.

3

The development of the model

This book is unique in aiming to provide teachers of primary school children with a model on which to base appraisal activities by means of self-evaluation. Thinking in terms of Squires' five dimensions, already explored in Figure 2.2, the *model* provides the *content* and the *justification*, the *school* provides the *context* and the *participants* and the *teacher* provides the *methods*.

The model is the result of the writer's own developing knowledge of possible ways of evaluating teacher effectiveness. This includes observing personally and on videos the interactions and daily events of several classrooms. It is also the 'product' of a series of meetings and exchange of correspondence and notes with many heads and teachers in different authorities who scrutinized and commented on several draft documents. The work finally resulted in the production of the model and its use in several schools.

Principles and rationales

The principle behind the model is a fairly simple one: it is essentially a specialized checklist of identified basic characteristics of the effective teacher of children in the three to eleven age range. It is organized into sections under the following headings:

1 Curriculum content.
2 Relationships with children.
3 Children's progress and achievements.
4 Discipline and child management.
5 Classroom administration, organization and display.
6 Teacher's professional attitudes and personality.

Against each statement contained within these sections, the teacher can rate herself, giving a personal estimate of her own strengths and weaknesses along a continuum. Information thus received is transferred to a histogram for ease of reference (Chapter 4 gives details).

Common sense rendered it vital to the busy class teacher that documented criteria for evaluation of effective teaching be kept as brief and succinct as possible. Certain features within the contents were thought to be vital in the light of personal and research contributions. These formed the basic rationales for the model and include the following:

1 The recognition that there is more to teaching than purely classroom practices. Inherent in all primary school teaching is the ability to care about the development of the 'whole' child. The teaching must be appropriate to this aim and the model must reflect this.

2 The ability of the model to assess only the effectiveness of the *teaching*. The research had to accept the notion of *learning* as the result of effective teaching and Section 3 (see Chapter 4), dealing with children's progress and achievements, is an attempt to maintain the links between teaching and learning.

Significantly, the work of Shields (1987–88), provides evidence of only four schools out of 31 whose expressed aim for teacher appraisal schemes is to improve children's education! No doubt questions will continue to be raised about the similarities and differences between teaching and learning. In primary education it is unlikely that any resolutions will easily be made. Any documented assessment of aspects of primary education suffers from being a quantitative approach to dealing with a qualitative situation.

However, some reference to how far the children are kept 'on-task' by the teacher appears to determine what they were learning (see Harnishfeger and Wiley, 1976, Galton *et al.*, 1980 and Galton and Simon, 1980). Similarly, the teacher's ability to ensure that children are appropriately matched to the level of the activities they are given (Bennett *et al.*, 1984).

3 The necessity for any criteria to be easily identifiable for teachers and translatable into their own classroom situations. The model also contains an inbuilt personalization element so that the dangers of over-generalization can be avoided.

4 The likelihood that assessment of certain items on the document are capable only of subjective judgements and, provided there is an awareness of this, it is acceptable. Total objectivity in a primary classroom is probably eternally elusive.

5 The need for at least some criteria to be directly observable in classroom/school situations. This would permit different perceptions of the same situation and responses to it to be explored.

6 The need for identification of constraints within the school environment and/or organization which would affect the effectiveness of the teachers within it. As pointed out by Salt (1985) 'the performance of any teacher can only be assessed with due regard to the ethos of the school as a whole'. (p. 22).

7 Brief mention made of the teacher's own capacity to learn. Progress in educational thinking is moving rapidly forward at present and teachers must be encouraged, if not to join the bandwagon, at least to analyse and review current issues and act and react according to personal views and those of immediate colleagues. In any case, knowing how to be a learner is a sombre but vital lesson for any teacher.

8 The belief that self-evaluation could, and probably should, lead to evaluation with or by others.

Aims and advantages

The main aim of this, as with any appraisal scheme, must be to increase a teacher's job satisfaction by identifying first, exactly what role the teacher is attempting to fulfil and secondly, how best the teacher can develop her full potential as an effective professional in that role. If staff feel dissatisfied with their 'lot', it is highly unlikely that the needs of the children will be met satisfactorily. Most primary school teachers have well-developed and internalized 'standards' and are not short on personal commitment. These tend still to be the chief motivating factors in work which retains its vocational nature. Fulfilment comes, therefore, with doing a fully satisfying job. Satisfaction is inherent in knowing what the parameters of the job are – and often doing more. What is important is not just what one is doing but what is being achieved.

The model also aims to provide opportunity for a variety of forms of assessment but takes self-evaluation as its mainstay. In 1985 Turner and Clift identified only three primary schools in this country where staff appraisal schemes of any kind were in operation. These were conducted almost entirely through interview and discussion with the head. Significantly by 1987–88, Shields had been able to locate 31 primary schools using some means of appraisal. Of these it appears that only eleven use any form of documentation as a starting point. Very few use self-evaluation as the main means to appraisal, most preferring appraisal interviews with the head and/or other senior colleagues.

The main advantages of this model have proved to be:

1 Its wide-ranging capabilities in providing opportunity for personalization of criteria within its own framework. Teachers are free, within their particular school context and situation, to amend or rephrase statements requiring further definition or explanation – to be explored in the next chapter.
2 Its strength in assessing (as at present) perceived teacher behaviours and the possibility of including observed teacher behaviours. The DES document 'Quality in Schools' (GB. DES, 1985) strongly supports observation as an essential part of any appraisal scheme.
3 Its potential in helping to identify in-service needs both in terms of individual teachers and whole staff, knowledge which could lead to better school-focused INSET which could well lead to better coordination of school policies and practices.
4 Its provision of a direct mechanism for a systematic planned programme of staff development which Rushby and Richards (1982) found extremely rare in primary schools.
5 The featuring of both summative and formative evaluation procedures, though mostly the latter. In other words, teachers can just self-evaluate and then stop (summative). However, the real value is that teachers can immediately identify what needs to be achieved in their own approach within the classroom in order to improve effectiveness (formative).
6 Its potential for highlighting the sheer amount of expertise now so necessary in coordinating primary school children's individual needs with curriculum require-ments yet still maintaining their learning of basic concepts and skills. These are not neglected in the model, the first section constituting a reminder that 'basic skills' are vital to effective learning and teaching.

What the model can, and cannot, do

There can be no doubt that the model has a simplicity of use which has been appreciated by teachers. It provides them with a means of gathering a wealth of information about themselves. Use of its contents on in-service courses has given another dimension to thinking. As the basis for teachers investigating the nature of their role and that of others it has been invaluable. In fact, this book is a result of many requests for more information on the model and its possible uses.

Like all documents related to subjective matters, the model tries to do too much; to be all things to all people. This, however, also gives it its flexibility. Used too bluntly, and without a knowledge of the stance it has taken and the essential in-built personalization factor, the document, rather than encouraging teacher creativity and experimentation in the learning process, could well stifle it. This danger must exist in the so-called 'Texas Test' brought in during 1986 – an examination undertaken by all the teachers in the state of Texas, determines whether or not they are competent to do their jobs. Failure (that is, a score under 75 per cent) results in dismissal. A blunt instrument for teacher appraisal by any standards and, given its contents (related to, among other things, pupil achievement and teacher's factual knowledge), one which takes little account of all the research previously discussed.

No attempt has been made to assess particularly effective methods or strategies except where they are implicit in effective teaching. It will be up to school staffs to include these in their discussions on staff appraisal. Winne (1977) observed that research on teacher effectiveness seldom does consider whether teacher behaviours or strategies influence learning differently for children having different abilities or preferences. This seems to be an equal failing of the present model.

To a certain extent, a major feature of primary education, the establishment of sound pupil–teacher relationships, has been underplayed in the model, mainly due to its very subjective nature. However, the quality of such relationships is highly apparent to the observer and, as observation is suggested as an integral part of teacher appraisal, this should be a self-cancelling criticism.

The model can only assess the effectiveness of the primary classroom teacher. Although attempts were made in the early stages to incorporate wording which would cover the appraisal of the role of the responsible post holder, this was clearly not possible within the existing model. A separate document would be required for each area of expertise and though, in all probability, many of the same elements would appear, such a document would need to dwell more in depth on managerial and relationship issues. Similarly, the model can only assess achieved competency. It proved unacceptable for student teachers in assessing potential competency in the classroom.

Finally, whatever the model contains, because it is setting precedents in an emotive field it is open to criticism. Equally, however, it is a feature of its time and is likely to be the forerunner of many other such documents.

Teachers' views of the model in use

The model was felt by teachers to focus on the job, be fair, objective, open and systematic, be easy to operate and emphasize development. Delaney (1986, p. 14) also found these factors to be vital to any scheme for teacher appraisal. Teachers were also pleased to have a model which evaluated them on their professional skills and abilities rather than on aspects like children's test results. It is significant that, at present, this issue is a real concern particularly to primary teachers.

Interestingly, teachers have also been motivated to see the model as the main aspect of an overall plan which would include:

1 The role of class teacher (identified by the model).
2 A particular job description for responsible post holders with a series of questions for the post holders to ask of themselves.
3 A year plan, termly forecast and review (both of children's and teacher's work).
4 A list of in-service needs identified and proposed with statements as to what the teacher would actually like to understand better at the end.

The model has frequently promoted reconsideration of schools' own curricular schemes and policy documents and generated new ones. Similarly, the staff in some schools have been prompted to review their practices of grouping children in the light of teachers' examining their practices in Sections 4 and 5 (see Chapter 4).

Of major importance has been the interactions between teachers generated by considerations of the model in use. Most teachers of primary age children spend a good deal of time thinking about and discussing their classroom practice and their groups of children. The model has acted as a focus for these discussions and helped teachers to see that their problems are indeed shared by many others!

Many teachers were surprised how much the model challenged some of their existing practices and thinking. Many were delighted that someone had finally documented the complexities of their task. Typical comments were:

> The document has given us much food for thought and has provoked considerable discussion which is a valuable end in itself.

> I feel this type of document can only be supportive to all teachers and keep us stretching out our goals all the time.

> Any teacher who fulfils half of these standards is, indeed, a 'pearl of great price'!

> Maybe we ought to give up teaching now!

It would probably be true to say that the effective teacher will be the one who has the courage and sense of professional responsibility to engage in self-evaluation. How the model may usefully be utilized for this purpose is now explained.

4

Undertaking self-evaluation: the means and the ends

First and foremost teachers must *want* to know about the effectiveness of their own classroom performance. Most do – many for personal reasons, some to see how they compare with others. Whatever the motives, the model provides structured statements for teachers to consider. However, this needs to be done systematically if the teacher is not to be overwhelmed. Before describing the processes involved in using the document, a few highlighted examples from within the six sections will assist teachers in gaining the most from their self-evaluation.

Section 1: Curriculum content

This section is essentially in two parts, the first one focusing on curriculum content and the second on putting the curriculum into practice. In addition to analysing the curriculum which she offers, the teacher must decide whether she provides within her classroom organization a variety of materials, apparatus and activities across a wide ability span which cover all areas of the identified curriculum. She must ask herself whether she allows plenty of opportunity for *all* children to take advantage of the materials, apparatus and activities provided as a learning resource. This sounds very obvious, but every teacher knows that certain children in the class can command attention to the detriment of others. There is also the necessity to look at the balance of what one might call the 'imposed' curriculum and the need for curriculum skills which grow from the child's interests and motivations. The questions of children's autonomy, developing independence opportunities for challenging play situations and purpose in learning are also raised here as vital issues in relation to curriculum considerations.

Section 2: Relationship with children

An expressed aim of just about all primary teachers must be to allow each child to develop to his or her own potential. This is very easily said and very difficult to achieve in a large class! This section tries to assist the teacher in emphasizing the many variables involved in looking at each individual learner and the many considerations such as sex, race and family background. Teachers must ask themselves really honestly whether they *do* offer all children similar opportunities as learners and also whether they offer all children equal amounts of teacher time and attention over different time spans. Teachers are also reminded of how much children are influenced by their peers particularly in the middle and upper primary ranges.

Section 3: Children's progress and achievements

The teacher's own plans for children's activities and learning together with records of achievement kept, provide the key to this section. A quick check would be to isolate one child at random and make a very brief profile of that child's current 'state of knowledge'. Do you really know him or her as well as you think? Does your subsequent teaching truly reflect the needs of that child, as well as all the others? Just as importantly, are you up-to-date with current thinking about how learning takes place and can you apply this to your class?

Section 4: Discipline and child management

Although no doubt all teachers would accept that making good relationships with children is at the heart of all control situations, there are particular strategies which can prevent difficulties arising. This section attempts to detail some of these tactics in the context of real awareness of what is happening in the classroom. Teachers should attempt occasionally to withdraw to the edge of the classroom and observe how the class appears to be operating both as a social system and in a practical context. When 'incidents' do occur, it is most helpful to consider what was happening just before, for example was the noise level rising rapidly, was the classroom routine disturbed, had the activities not been explained clearly to the children?

Section 5: Classroom administration, organization and display

Although lumped together these are, in fact, very different skills – an excellent administrator can sometimes see little need for good display. However, it is unlikely that an untidy, messy and noisy classroom is the ideal climate for quiet, on-task learning. In 5(h) teachers will quickly recognize whether they feel constantly harrassed by lack of time (given that there is never enough of it). Similarly, do children have to climb over one another to retrieve materials they need? Are quiet activities placed next to noisy ones? Are messy activities located where human 'traffic' is at its greatest. Small features but quite capable of causing chaos in an ill-planned environment.

Section 6: Teacher's professional attitudes and personality

Issues of teaching personality are always emotive. Yet few of us would doubt that certain characteristics such as a sense of humour are really quite vital in becoming an effective teacher, not least because an ability to laugh *with* the children can often release a lot of tension in the classroom for everyone! However, the type of teacher you are has equal ramifications beyond the classroom. Teachers are part of a larger team and a wider community and they cannot fulfil their duties to the children without considerations of these. This section outlines some of these duties and responsibilities.

A glance at the section headings will no doubt create questions immediately! Why do curriculum matters occur before relationships with children? Most primary school teachers would feel that the latter is of the most vital importance and should always be considered first. Others may feel that teaching personality and attitudes determine the effectiveness of the individual. In practice, it is not important in what order these headings occur but rather that they do occur, to identify the main features covered by the model. Many other headings were possible but, in any document of this type, a stance has to be taken which inevitably restricts areas to those felt most vital by the participants.

Teachers may argue whether equal weighting is attached to each section. Although the very nature of sectioning suggests discrete categories, this is not the case. Much overlap and interrelationship occur between the various criteria and sections. Teachers can confidently take the sections in any order and find a variety of classroom life represented there.

When to use the model

The model may be used at any time when a need is identified for assessing the effective teaching of either individuals or whole school staffs. At best, this will be when teachers have a genuine interest in finding out what their individual strengths are and where in-service training needs lie. The stimulus should ideally come from the teachers themselves or from a school-inspired system of teacher appraisal agreed by all parties (though there is, of course, the possibility of government legislation which could enforce teacher appraisal as part of contractual duties). One strength of the model is that self-evaluation can begin at any time in the school year, when needs manifest themselves.

How to use the model

The format of the model, as can be seen in Appendix C, comprises for each section a page of criteria statements followed by a blank page for personalized comments (in the case of Section 1 there are two such pages). The six sections allow the opportunity for one to be taken and worked on for each half-term in the school year. A suggested mode of operation would be as follows.

1 After a careful study of the section's contents, a teacher would review her performance in relation to *each individual criterion* within a particular section. The best way to do this is to work on a 'rating' for each item on a 1–10 scale in pencil. For example, if she considers herself to excel in each aspect, her rating would be 10. In the unlikely event of her being totally inadequate, her rating would be 1. Most teachers will find themselves somewhere between these extremes.

It is then necessary to add up all the numbers so achieved and divide the total by the number of items in the section. As an example, if within Section 2 the total score turned out to be 75, this divided by 15 items would give a score of 5, that is half way along the continuum. This then gives the overall rating for that section. Still in pencil, this rating is then transferred to the continuum at the appropriate point. This exercise will also reveal where personalization of the statements is needed.

The exercise is a three-fold one in that it needs:

(a) Quiet undisturbed time (probably at home!) to digest the contents.

(b) Time made during the busy day within the classroom to observe those features which can only be objectively evaluated in this way.

(c) Time set aside while working with children to monitor the level and suitability of the tasks on which they are engaged and assess progress.

2 The teacher will then consider her own school situation and note, under 'Personal comments', any features which are particular to her class or school context. These will include such aspects as those identified on pages 8 and 8a of the model and possibly others specific to different schools.

3 She should then review her original rating in the light of the personalized statements and ink in her final decision immediately. *This is important.* Reflection will and should occur later. Also, the longer the time span on decisions the more opportunity there is for other variables to intervene and distract from the original exercise. A completed sample page is shown in Table 4.1.

4 This process is then repeated for each of the remaining five sections.

5 The completed ratings from all six sections should then be transferred to the histogram on page 9 of the model. As can be seen from Figure 4.1 this now represents a profile of that teacher's self-evaluation.

Analysis of findings

In the light of this profile, the teacher will be able to decide:

1 what she is doing effectively;
2 where her strengths lie;
3 where her weaknesses lie and therefore what in-service requirements she has;
4 what modifications are needed in classroom practices;
5 the issues which she perhaps needs to take up with the head teacher or other colleagues.

At this point the teacher will probably also feel the need to make some notes regarding her thoughts on the balance of the histogram produced. It is quite possible and reasonable to make notes directly on to the model as reminders of earlier thinking. Other questions which she might consider at this point would be:

1 what aspects of the job have given the greatest satisfaction this year?
2 what aspects have given least satisfaction?
3 have I any abilities which are not being fully used?
4 what experiences/help do I now need to become a better teacher;
5 what gives me confidence that I am 'growing' in the job I do?
6 have I any new abilities, knowledge, attitudes or skills which I can incorporate into my role next year?
7 what are likely to be my major constraints and how can I prepare for them?

The teacher should then decide whether the opinion of a peer or senior colleague would be useful. Most of us find it easier to order our thoughts more efficiently in discussion with another person and bounce some ideas off against them in order to come to terms with our own thinking. It may also be that, as observation is deemed by many including the DES to be an integral factor in appraisal, the teacher may ask a colleague to observe some aspects included in the model. Sections 2 and 4 particularly contain elements where an outside opinion might be useful.

Moving on

Having made the self-evaluation, certain things will have become apparent, as shown in Figure 4.1. It may be that on one particular section (in this case Section 2), a teacher has

Table 4.1: Completing a section of the model

Section 2: Relationship with children	Personal comments

In relating to children, I am able to:

(a) Recognize and enhance the need in every child for a positive self-image ⑤ *I try!* ⑥

(b) Acknowledge and encourage children's ideas and contributions to activities. ④ *Too many children!* ④

(c) Interact with individual children every day. ⑧ ⑧

(d) Thoroughly understand the personality needs of individuals and groups of children. ⑤ ⑤

(e) Participate in activities alongside children. ⑧ ⑧

(f) Understand when and when not to intervene in children's tasks. ⑧ ⑧

(g) Communicate with children easily in verbal and non-verbal situations. ④ *Language 'problems' in this class / E2L* ⑤

(h) Recognize the growing influence of the peer group on children's attitudes and behaviour. ③ *Need to read up on this!* ③

(i) Be essentially positive and encouraging in all dealings with children. ⑤ ⑤

(j) Provide a suitable adult 'model' for children. ⑨ ⑨

(k) Make myself aware of child's background and other relevant information. ⑥ *Try hard! Can head help?* ⑤

(l) Use a variety of types of questioning to elicit thoughtful responses. ② *How can I ask more 'open' questions?* ②

(m) Make time to listen to children. ⑤ *As much as I can with 35!!* ④

(n) Recognize the need for awareness of equal opportunities for boys and girls. ④ *Cultural difficulties* ④

(o) Recognize the need for awareness of equal opportunities for children from all ethnic and cultural backgrounds. ④ *Many ethnic backgrounds to cope with* ④
5·3
15│80

Need to read up on open questioning + peer groups
See head re E2L children + backgrounds

1 → 2 → 3 → 4 → 5 → 6 → 7 → 8 → 9 → 10
Very inadequate   **5·3**   Excellent

Figure 4.1: Completing the histogram

Histogram related to the level of effectiveness of the teacher as identified within the section of the model

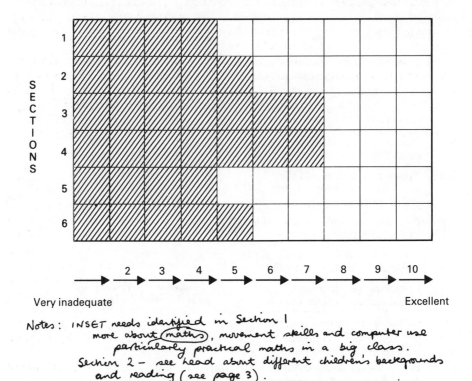

Very inadequate   Excellent

Notes: INSET needs identified in Section 1.
more about (maths), movement skills and computer use
particularly practical maths in a big class.
Section 2 - see head about different children's backgrounds
and reading (see page 3).
Section 5 - sort out my groupings better - reorganise
classroom - what do I need?
Section 6 - need to make more time to talk to other staff!

scored rather poorly but on other aspects she feels much more confident. On the other hand, a number of needs may have been identified across several sections. The teacher will have to decide on some order of priority. In general the writer would recommend that this priority list does not make the very weakest aspect the immediate focus of attention, something which can be rather demoralizing. This is *not* the object of the exercise. Teachers should begin with anything which is of real interest to them and is something they genuinely would like to work at or know more about. This then becomes the teachers' 'developmental programme'.

It may be that this priority list will require revision according to the in-service provision available within any given school term and year. It may also be that this priority list matches that of other teachers and decisions are made to make some in-school, in-service provision in these areas. The onset of provision under grant related in-service training (GRIST) money has opened up wide-ranging possibilities for schools and teachers and should enhance opportunities for requisite in-service education when it is fully underway.

Whatever the ordering of the priority list, teachers must not feel overly pressurized as this can only affect their relationships within the classroom and school. They must feel that they are out to achieve worthwhile objectives. An interspersion of short- and long-term objectives is also helpful. A day in the classroom will leave most teachers feeling fairly exhausted! Even if in-service takes place in school time, the responsibility to the children never quite goes away. In all probability, much of a teacher's in-service education will still take place out of school hours and several on-going evening sessions will drain even the hardiest.

Dilemmas in interpretation of statements contained within the documents will usefully be resolved in consultation with colleagues. Uncertainty in knowing what to do about problems identified could be resolved in similar discussion with colleagues or perhaps by making reference to relevant literature (the selected bibliography, pp. 37–40, suggests texts which teachers may find helpful in this regard).

If a three-year cycle of self-evaluation is operated the teacher would undertake the self-evaluation using the model in year one, have years two and three to undertake appropriate in-service education and return to the model at the beginning of year four to begin the process again. Comparisons with the previous evaluation could then be made at the end of each half term or could be left for analysis until the year's end when decisions on the next two years needs are made.

Time factors

This makes it all sound rather a lengthy process. In reality, teachers need spend only about three to four hours over a year on familiarizing themselves with the model and rating their effectiveness. About another hour is needed for deciding on priorities and organizing thinking on aspects of in-service provision. This compares well with the Suffolk study of 1985 already mentioned in Chapter 1. The main conclusions of the study were that, although justified by results, a national scheme would be costly in time and personnel, as much as 12 hours per teacher per year being required. As teachers are undoubtedly the most expensive resource of the education system, any amount of time spent enhancing effectiveness could probably be justified. Such expenditure of time, however useful, would be questioned by a majority of teachers who see the time spent with the children as being of most value.

Of course time will need to be built into the school day for observations and possibilities of working with small groups of children. In the writer's experience, these types of activities take place when another teacher, or the head, has the majority of the class for story, singing or the like. This actually serves a useful hidden function in limiting the time available, which in turn concentrates teachers' attentions on the task in hand.

The 1986 Education Act recommends biennial appraisal. The writer and teachers who helped to develop the model feel that this gives insufficient time for teachers to get to grips with developing their skills given the present in-service arrangements. Teachers must be able to see real progress as the results of their labours – three years gives time for this to become evident. Perhaps changes in in-service provision could create a justifiable reduction in this time.

One further point regarding the section on constraints. It would be very easy to make these the basis of excuses for not operating effectively or not actually following up the evaluation. The reality is that we all work under different constraints and it is by recognizing them for what they are – difficulties not straightjackets – that we minimize them. Teachers are an innovative group of people and usually find the will and means to overcome problems with good humour.

A few conclusions so far

A job description such as the model provides benefits by on-going discussion in relation to its contents and use. This means that even as a self-evaluation document teachers must at least discuss these aspects if not their own particular outcomes. In this way the model will evolve just as the education system around us is evolving all the time. Using the model, priorities will change from year to year, but the model itself provides a stability of thinking that many teachers have desired for some time. A regular worry heard in schools relates to the state of flux in which teachers constantly find themselves and the ever-changing nature of what they do. Most feel they are running to stand still much of the time. This in turn affects the way they view themselves and their own effectiveness as teachers. The situation is complex and difficult to change. It is certainly highly correlated with having your 'worth' acknowledged. Most people work twice as hard if they feel valued.

'Quality in Schools' (1985), acknowledges that 'a healthy perception of status and good morale are critical and need to be actively sought for' (paragraph 139) but like so many government documents of this kind it does not suggest *how* this may be achieved.

It is obviously important that a teacher's self-image as a professional is not only maintained but heightened by the experience of appraisal. The hope is that disillusioned or disheartened teachers will see from the identification of criteria contained in the model, that much of what they do is truly valuable.

Warwick (1983) and Gould (1984) both suggest that a sense of worth is attainable through appraisal interviews with a senior colleague where objectives are set and tasks clearly defined. The model has obvious uses in this direction. Some teachers will be unhappy in having the full responsibility for evaluation of their effectiveness. Some may even fool themselves into believing that everything is quite satisfactory. Self-evaluation plus assessment by 'another' would seem a reasonable system provided the two people involved combine to interpret their joint findings. This and other possible advances from self-evaluation are the subject of the next chapter.

5

Self-evaluation – the way forward

On the question of who should do the appraising the majority preferred to be appraised by themselves (self-evaluation), a person nominated by them and a senior colleague. (Lusty, 1983, p. 374).

The teachers' responses as to who should appraise, mirror almost exactly those quoted above, yet teachers using the model have actually been quite hard on themselves. Perhaps this is a characteristic of people striving to do better? Using the model with another peer colleague has often meant earlier harsh views of the self being moderated. This must be advantageous for individuals who gain the knowledge that respected colleagues are appreciative of the job they do. Most of us feel reasonably happy if we can tell ourselves that we have done a good job. The satisfaction is definitely increased, however, if someone else tells us we have.

The very nature of the job means that teachers cannot operate in a vacuum. Opportunities now occur in many primary schools for others to be involved in classroom practice, both those directly employed within education and others such as parents. Particularly in nursery, early primary education and open-plan situations, teachers frequently work with both parallel colleagues and with nursery nurses and ancillaries. This system is ideal for the teaching group to get together, decide on a section of the model to be considered and observe and monitor each other in particular situations. Not all teachers have this opportunity. Yet as teachers we must recognize what it is like to be learners, so that we realize what expectations we can have of the children. We must talk about what we do, why we do it and constantly learn from each other.

The relatively 'open' situation of many primary schools makes them ideal places from which to begin this kind of project. It may involve appraisal at all levels and across hierarchies. School use of the document may well engender a spirit of collective responsibility – an effective team is likely to be comprised of effective individuals. Therefore, although constituting an appraisal document, the model would actually enhance a feeling of corporate professional worth.

All this, however, depends upon each individual's perception of self matching the perceptions of others. Let us look at some of the issues.

Matching perceptions

Needless to say this is a very sensitive issue and schools are not always so open to the kind of honesty required. It really does require teachers to delve into practices and beliefs, examination of which can be extremely uncomfortable. We all do things we have done for years simply because we *have* done them for years. Often they are practices adopted for our own convenience and do not necessarily reflect what the children really need. The arguments about what is good for the teacher must be good for the children holds some measure of acceptability but practices have often ceased even to be really helpful for the teacher and yet are pursued irrespectively.

One of the best ways for a school staff to use the model is to adopt it as the basis for a series of staff meetings. One a half-term regarding each section fits neatly into the school year. The purpose of such meetings would be the following.

1 To begin to discuss teacher appraisal in an unthreatening way, voluntarily, before external pressures dictate practice.
2 To establish a core of ideas about what constitutes effective primary teaching.
3 To establish a common ground in relation to subjective phraseology, i.e. what is considered by the group collectively to be 'appropriate', 'suitable', 'good knowledge', and so on.
4 To personalize the document in relation to the school as a whole. Individual teachers could operate their own personalization in relation to their class of children.
5 To decide on a procedure for collective or individual use of the document.

In this way at least individual school staffs may begin the process of self-evaluation and teacher appraisal and coordinate a shared philosophy. It also becomes patently clear that each will be assessed by fair and consistent means.

Heads, senior colleagues and peer colleagues – not to mention HMI advisers and local education authority personnel – will all have their own unique perceptions of what the role of the teacher (as well as their own) entails. Their interpretations of different situations and expectations will differ. Within the school this would hopefully be minimal if the staff as a whole are used to discussing issues and practices. If they are not, their views could differ widely from the teacher's own.

If other educationalists' perceptions of the teacher do differ significantly from her own, she must consider what this means in relation to self-evaluation, staff appraisal interview systems and accountability. What must also be borne in mind is that other more educationally naive people, with yet different perceptions, also rate what you do. Consider parents as an example. What evidence do they have on which to judge schools' and teachers' performance? First, they have the 'grapevine' and the evidence of their own eyes (more powerful indicators than perhaps any of us realize). Such aspects include:

1 a teacher's dress and general demeanour;
2 the comments of their own and other children;
3 the comments of other parents;
4 observations of the teacher in the company of children, i.e. playground, school, outside visits;
5 the comments of ancillaries and helpers;
6 media coverage of teachers' activities.

Other indicators for parents would include:

1 the tone and content of notes, newsletters, information sent home;
2 the quality of meetings with teachers to discuss children's progress;
3 to what extent the teachers seem to care about the school and its reputation;
4 the work children take home;
5 the responses teachers make to parents' inquiries;
6 attendance at concerts, plays, open days.

A more comprehensive list is included in the 1979 East Sussex Accountability Project.

Evaluation of the teacher may be made from all these sources and we ignore them at our peril! Governors again will have their own perceptions of teachers gleaned from different sources and, with their increasing powers, they could well become involved in teacher appraisal to quite a great extent. The roles of some of these people in a teacher's self-evaluation are now explored.

Involving the head and senior colleagues

In all the appraisal schemes collated by Shields (1987–88), an appraisal interview with the head is an integral part. Sometimes these are very informal with no documentation preceding or succeeding the session. Teachers who used the present model found it an ideal tool through which to discuss their performance and future needs with the head at yearly intervals. They and the head benefited by already having clearly stated the role of a primary class teacher and what items particular to that school aided or hindered their effectiveness. The developmental programme decided upon by the teacher also assisted the head in deciding upon in-school in-service requirements. Where senior colleagues with special responsibilities were also included, this led to systematic planning for school needs. For example, if teachers felt they were ineffective in dealing with a particular curriculum aspect, this perhaps meant revision of the school scheme currently in operation. If several teachers report the same problems at successive appraisal interviews, this has obvious repercussions for future staff meetings.

The model makes it possible for heads to respond to the appraisal of teachers in several ways, in addition to promoting staff meeting discussions.

1 Heads may use the teacher's self-evaluation as the basis for a staff appraisal interview, the purpose of which would be to assess where the teacher is now in terms of level of knowledge and expertise. By this means the head would gain a profile of each member of staff's possible contribution. Most heads find these interviews helpful in getting to know their staffs as individual people and in establishing a trusting relationship. In Shields' (1987–88) research appraisal interviews with heads formed the basis of almost all the schemes identified.

2 Heads may accept the teacher's self-evaluation and use it as the basis for establishing a report on present levels of achievement and job satisfaction, the teacher's strengths and future goals. The latter may involve discussion and advice on promotion prospects and career development generally. Paramount in all such documentation is the confidentiality of any reports produced between the two parties. Outside parties are only involved by agreement on both sides.

3 Heads may decide to undertake an independent evaluation of the teacher using the model, either personally or by delegating a senior colleague. Results of the teacher's self-evaluation and the head's evaluation may then be used as the basis for an appraisal interview. This is useful in developing agreed perceptions but takes longer than the first method. Inherent in this method would also be the need for the designated senior colleague to undertake observation of the teacher's performance in the classroom. This point will be taken up in more detail below.

4 Heads may decide to ask a group of teachers, perhaps a particular year group, to evaluate their combined teaching, highlighting certain sections of the model and report back as a group. This enables the head and a group of teachers to gain some common perceptions of school practices with specific age groups.

The teachers who were part of the original research saw appraisal with the head or a senior colleague as by far the most acceptable form after self-evaluation (see Appendix A, p. 42). This view appears to have something to do with the generally hierarchical nature of schools and the fact that ultimately the head is responsible for all the personnel and policies. After senior colleague appraisal, peer group involvement was also welcomed. The model has been used in a variety of ways in this context.

Involving peer colleagues

Probably the first and the hardest thing to realize is that using a friend to assist with self-evaluation is usually unwise! Friends find it especially difficult to be really objectively critical of colleagues as they will often know of factors beyond the school which will influence how they consider their colleague's school performance. Other people could well be critical of the outcomes of such an appraisal which they would inevitably feel biased because of the friendship. A reciprocal arrangement, with a trusted but critical colleague, for assisting with self-evaluation is by far the most reliable. The two parties need to be very honest with each other, respect each other as professionals and feel confident that each has an informed and objective view of the process. On most school staffs it is possible for individuals to find such a colleague. This will occur more especially if schools have undertaken whole staff meetings to discuss the process and effects of teacher appraisal and self-evaluation.

As with the senior colleague appraisal, there are various options to pursue.

1 One teacher discussing with the other her self-evaluation and seeking confirmation and comment on her findings. The main points of the discussion can be turned into a report which could then support discussions with the head or others regarding the teacher's performance and needs.

2 Each may independently complete the information on the model both for themselves and for their colleague. This will inevitably require some time spent together in each other's classrooms as well as time to discuss their mutual findings. Heads are usually only too happy, if arrangements are made in good time, to release teachers by whatever means available to them, for the purpose of mutual appraisal. (A coin tossed will decide which teacher is selected for attention first!) This usually results in teachers also monitoring the effects of the decisions made through on-going discussions.

3 Within this category it may or may not be the case that particular responsibility post holders are peer colleagues. If this is indeed the case, and the teacher's self-evaluation reveals weakness in, say, mathematics teaching, she may well decide to seek the support and guidance of the maths coordinator as her peer appraiser.

4 Alternatively, and sometimes a better arrangement, might be for one school to pair up with another and exchange teachers who then have a more independent view of the school in which they find themselves. Particularly with small schools, clustering has become quite a common occurrence, as have exchanges of expertise. This would then become another acceptable system within a system, but as yet has not been attempted with this particular model or process as far as the writer knows.

5 Teachers may wish to share their self-evaluations with a group of peers and form self-help groups within the school. This has the added advantage of allowing teachers to share not only common perceptions but common problems as well! This situation has also served to alleviate too much reliance on the model and focus more sharply on practices. If these self-help groups span year group teaching within the school so much the better. At all levels of teaching we must value more greatly the stages

before and after our own current age group of children. Respect for teachers of other age groups can be greatly increased through appraisal discussions.

Teachers will no doubt think of many more ways of sharing their interpretations and perceptions with colleagues, to the benefit of all, including the model.

Involving others

At present the model has not been used with those outside the immediate school situation. The following, therefore, is speculative though worthy of mention in the current ever-changing educational climate.

While at present it seems that the government is satisfied to press local authorities, and through them schools, to formulate staff appraisal systems, many other people have a vested interest in teacher appraisal. Most authorities have insufficient primary school advisers for them to adopt more than a professional interest in appraisal although many, in the writer's experience, have a profound interest in particularly those aspects which serve to promote professional development. Sallis (1983) and Midwinter (1985) both suggest that insufficient attention has been paid to parents and governors as possible assessors of teachers' effectiveness and point out that it is normally quite obvious to them if an ineffective teacher operates within their school milieu. Sallis particularly feels that governors should be more directly involved in schools' own attempts at teacher evaluations than they currently appear to be. Green (1981) suggests that HMI, with its high professional ideals, is nearer to providing a 'proper professional channel of accountability for teachers as anything' (p. 43).

Last, but certainly not least, are the children. Pupil ratings of teachers have been used particularly in the USA with older pupils, but perhaps primary children are too emotional in their relationships with teachers, and too inexperienced, to judge effectively. Work done by the writer, however, has suggested that, even as young as six, children are able to discuss the value of the activities they undertake. Perhaps insufficient credit is given to young children's ability to estimate the worth of the tasks they so willingly undertake for the teacher's sake (see Bennett et al., 1984). Perhaps this is another way for individual items on the model to be examined.

Whether self-evaluation is the key means to teacher appraisal or any of the other forms discussed so far, without classroom observations the exercise will fall short of being totally satisfactory.

Observation of the teacher 'in action'

In these technological days, self-evaluation *can* be accompanied by observation of oneself in the classroom. This means, of course, by use of video. Video is unique in giving time for re-run and reflection in a way that the busy classroom cannot. Teachers who have not seen themselves in action are strongly urged to try to do so – a salutary experience but a most worthwhile one! At last the opportunity now exists for 'the giftie . . . to see oursels as others see us' (Robert Burns, *To a Louse*). If schools do not have their own equipment, this procedure can often be facilitated by teachers' centres, local colleges and universities and, sometimes, interested secondary schools.

Much of the earlier work on the model's contents was developed through analysing video films of teachers in the classroom. In several schools, the teacher in focus allowed the film to be used for staff discussion purposes and this, too, proved invaluable.

To answer particular questions such as 'How does the teacher actually spend her time in the classroom?', time-lapse filming has been useful. The camera actually takes a number of frames focused on the teacher for one minute in every five. At the end of a five hour school day, this gives approximately one hour of film showing the basis of the teacher's day and interactions during it.

Other uses of video would include filming the teacher in a whole-class session or group sessions. This would provide information on a number of items in the model, e.g. Section 2, items (b), (c), (e), (f), (g), (i), (l) and Section 4, items (b), (d), (e), (f), (i), (j), (m), (n), (o).

Conclusions

Personal observation of the teacher by either a senior colleague or a peer colleague is probably the most practical and easy to organize. It is also the one in most common use as part of appraisal using the model. It has the benefit of providing on-the-spot responses to particular features of classroom life and teaching skills. It has the hidden advantage of taking the appraiser into another teacher's classroom. Most are complimentary regarding what they see as they know only too well the difficulties of the situation, i.e. one teacher often to 30 or more children!

The writer is in a privileged position in being able to visit many classrooms in different schools. The overwhelming impression is that teachers almost expect 'visitors' to be critical of classroom practices. They tend to feel that somehow their classes should be doing something else whenever others are around – though they never seem sure what! This appears to stem from many sources, not least of which are the many complexities of the job and the fact that teachers are really very autonomous in their own classrooms. They rarely see other teachers at work and, therefore, have no situations by which to evaluate their own teaching. Perhaps, as suggested by Bassey (1980), these attitudes are 'indicative of the awesome nature of teaching children' (p. 17).

Use of the model as a structure determined by equal professionals helps to allay some of these fears. After all, the particular teacher under observation today could well be the observer in another classroom tomorrow. Teachers involved in developing the model were greatly encouraged by seeing other teachers in action. Experience of in-service courses where teachers are given the opportunity to visit other schools, suggests to the writer that these visits are the highlight of the teachers' experiences. The more classroom observation becomes an integral part of school life, the more teachers will value its uses and accept its consequences – and value associated systems.

6

Finale: drawing it all together

From an original perceived need in one particular school and a national incentive generated almost simultaneously, appraisal has become *the* contentious issue of the late 1980s. Breaking new ground at such a time, the model has been remarkably well received. This probably stems from its total involvement of practising teachers from the outset. This involvement arose from a genuine interest in, and determination to come to terms with, the whole process of teacher appraisal and, in particular, self-evaluation. Many teachers appear to welcome some form of appraisal, if only to quell public anxieties regarding contemporary education, but are quite rightly concerned to have a hand in deciding the form it should take.

It would be easy to be critical of such a model emerging, as it does, at a time when teachers are being asked to account for themselves in public and professional ways perhaps as never before. The question of what skills, attributes and processes make for effective primary teaching will, no doubt, be reiterated over and over again in the coming months and years. As Lusty (1983) suggests, 'The day of reckoning for teachers is speeding onwards, if it has not already arrived' (p. 377).

In making clear what primary teachers do, we allow them to justify their role to others in and out of teaching. Without such a definition of effectiveness, primary teachers have, in the past, often defended rather than justified, their role. This has led to situations of conflict in education and created atmospheres which are not conducive to children's learning. After all what is teacher appraisal about if it is not the improvement of learning possibilities for children? Significantly, responses from schools regarding the purpose of their appraisal systems in Shields' (1987–88) research, produced only six out of 31 heads who stated any objectives in terms of children's learning. This is clearly a case where one issue is clouding the consideration of another. The benefits to the children, or for that matter the teachers, are certainly not immediately and directly observable. If, however, one considers the following points made by teachers using the document, the hidden advantages become clear.

1 Using the model, particularly with others, emphasized the importance of teachers as *people*.
2 Greater trust and understanding was generated between colleagues.
3 Mutual support has brought some of the joys of its vocational nature back to the job of teaching.
4 The contents of the model made teachers realize the importance and complexity of the job they do, thus raising morale.
5 Professional development and strengths are emphasized where so often in recent years appraisal has been equated with negative features such as reduction of salary or status or even loss of the teaching post.

6 The model facilitates communication in what could otherwise be a relatively threatening concept.
7 Practices are critically but objectively reviewed in the context of the classroom and in relation to what the document identifies as the role of the effective primary teacher.

In the (now defunct) DES magazine, *Trends* (1977), the editorial said

> Not all teachers are, or ever will be, the best teachers anyone could wish, but all teachers should be given the tools and training to become the best teachers that they individually can be. To have such teachers is at the very least the right of every child.

The writer would add that to *be* such a teacher is the right of all of us. Any document which can help teachers towards these goals must be welcomed by the profession.

The present situation of unease in schools is hardly a propitious climate for any constructive thinking into teacher appraisal schemes. Similarly, at a time when a radical restructuring of the major features of the system is being considered (or should we say, being steam-rollered!) teacher appraisal based on teaching as it is currently conceived may seem inappropriate. At present we cannot know the long term effects that self-evaluation or any other means of appraisal with have on the teachers. We can speculate, however, that systems based on practices and processes which teachers themselves have identified are most likely to succeed.

Constant and on-going 'talking' about appraisal without any action ensuing only increases and heightens teachers' discomfort with the proposals. This model documents a great deal of what is presently only talk. Similarly, action must follow needs identified through use of the model for self-evaluation. The role of others in the evaluation must essentially be to assist individual teachers in the process of solving their own problems.

Looking to the future

So what of the future of teacher appraisal? Quite obviously, where teacher appraisal is going is dependent upon where the education system itself is going. At this time of rapid change, speculation on this issue abounds but answers are sparce and tentative at best. Any form of appraisal will involve time, money and commitment. Time and money are always at a premium in education, particularly in the primary phase. The training and experience of appraisers by any means other than self-evaluation will be a very costly and contentious issue and the question of who should appraise, if not the individual teacher, is riddled with problems. Answers are in short supply at present. Unpleasant and daunting tasks such as deciding upon grievance procedures would be only one of many major concerns and may possibly involve resources best used for promoting the children's education more directly. Time and money will still need to be spent on the training of teachers on how best to achieve competent self-evaluation but at least these are likely to have direct and positive repercussions for the children. Hopefully both will be available in good quantity if the government and LEAs are intent on developing a system of excellence.

Hierarchical teacher appraisal schemes are 'management' inspired and threatening. At worst, they are devisive, destructive and promote a retreat by teachers into the known and comfortable. They could obliterate innovative and flexible primary teaching and create a digging-in of heels such as contemporary education has not seen before. Harsh words, maybe: words indicative of the strong feelings of some teachers, they certainly are.

Self-evaluation requires even greater professional commitment than an imposed hierarchical appraisal scheme. The writer believes that primary teachers are well skilled in coping with the autonomy implied by self-evaluation. The present model provides them with the necessary structure to begin.

References

AULD, R. (1976). *William Tyndale Junior and Infants School: Public Enquiry* (The Auld Report). London: ILEA.

BARR, A. S. (1961). 'Wisconsin studies of the measurement and prediction of teacher effectiveness – a summary of investigations', *The Journal of Experimental Education*, 30, 1, 1–155.

BARROW, R. (1984). *Giving Teaching Back to Teachers*. Brighton: Wheatsheaf Books.

BASSEY, M. (1980). Trent Papers in Education. Nottingham: Trent Polytechnic.

BECHER, A., ERAUT, M. and KNIGHT, J. (1982). 'Policy options at the school level'. In: MCCORMICK, R. (Ed) *Calling Education to Account*. London: Heinemann Educational.

BENNETT, S. N., DESFORGES, C., COCKBURN, A. and WILKINSON, B. (1984). *The Quality of Pupil Learning Experiences*. New Jersey: Lawrence Erlbaum.

BERLINGER, D. (1976). 'Impediments to the study of teacher effectiveness', *Journal of Teacher Education*, 27, 1, 5–13.

BRITTON, J. (1969). 'Talking to learn'. In: BARNES, D., BRITTON, J. and ROSEN, H. (Eds) *Language, the Learner and the School*. Harmondsworth: Penguin.

DEAN, J. (1982). 'Evaluation and advisers'. In: MCCORMICK, R. *Calling Education to Account, op.cit.*

DELANEY, P. (1986). *Teacher Appraisal in the Primary School: One School's Experience*. Junior Education Special Report. Leamington Spa: Scholastic Publications.

DENHAM, C. and LIEBERMAN, A. (1980). *Time to Learn*. Washington, DC: National Institute of Education.

DOMAS, S. J. and TIEDEMAN, D. V. (1950). 'Teacher competence. An annotated bibliography', *Journal of Experimental Education*, 19, 2, 101–218.

DOYLE, K. D. (1983). *Evaluating Teaching*. Lexington, Mass: Lexington Books.

DUNKIN, M. J. and BIDDLE, B. J. (1974). *The Study of Teaching*. New York: Holt Rinehart.

DUTHIE, J. H. (1972). 'A study of the teacher's day'. In: MORRISON, M. and MCINTYRE, D. *The Social Psychology of Teaching*. Harmondsworth: Penguin.

EAST SUSSEX ACCOUNTABILITY PROJECT (1979). *Accountability in the Middle Years of School*. Self-published policy document.

ELLIOTT, J. (1973–75). *Developing Hypotheses about Classrooms From Teachers' Practical Constructs*. Unit 1. Cambridge: Ford Teaching Project.

ELLIOTT, J. and ADELMAN, C. (1973–75). *The Innovation Process in the Classroom*. Unit 3. Cambridge: Ford Teaching Project.

EVERTSON, C. M. and BROPHY, J. E. (1974). *The Texas Teacher Effectiveness Project*. Washington, DC: National Institute of Education.

FLANDERS, N. W. (1970). *Analysing Teaching Behaviour*. Boston, Mass: Addison Wesley.

GAGE, N. L. (1963). *Handbook of Research on Teaching*. Chicago: Rand McNally.

GAGNE, R. M. (1970). *The Conditions of Learning*, 2nd edn. New York: Holt, Rinehart & Winston.

GALTON, M. and SIMON, B. (1980). *Progress and Performance in the Primary Classroom*. London: Routledge & Kegan Paul.

GALTON, M., SIMON, B. and CROLL, P. (1980). *Inside the Primary Classroom*. London: Routledge & Kegan Paul.

GOULD, G. (1984). 'Measuring teacher performance', *Education*, 163, 16, 238.

GREAT BRITAIN. DEPARTMENT OF EDUCATION AND SCIENCE (1972). *Trends*. London: HMSO.

GREAT BRITAIN. DEPARTMENT OF EDUCATION AND SCIENCE (1977). 'Ten Good Schools'. London: DES Green Paper.

GREAT BRITAIN. DEPARTMENT OF EDUCATION AND SCIENCE (1982). 'Teaching Quality'. London: DES White Paper.

GREAT BRITAIN. DEPARTMENT OF EDUCATION AND SCIENCE (1985). 'Better Schools: A Summary'. London: HMSO.

GREAT BRITAIN. DEPARTMENT OF EDUCATION AND SCIENCE (1985). 'Quality in Schools: Evaluation and Appraisal'. London: HMSO.

GREAT BRITAIN. DEPARTMENT OF EDUCATION AND SCIENCE (1986). Education Act. London: HMSO.

GREAT BRITAIN. DEPARTMENT OF EDUCATION AND SCIENCE (1987). Education Act. London: HMSO.

GREAT BRITAIN. DEPARTMENT OF EDUCATION AND SCIENCE (1987). 'Primary Schools: Some Aspects of Good Practice'. London: HMSO.

GREEN, C. (1981). 'Teacher's accountability: towards a quality profession?', Education, 9, 3–13.

HARNISHFEIGER, A. and WILEY, D. E. (1976). 'Teaching–learning processes in the elementary school: a synoptic view'. Beginning Teacher Evaluation Study, Technical Report, 75–3–1, San Francisco, Calif.

INNER LONDON EDUCATION AUTHORITY (ILEA) (1983). Set of video tapes. Meeting Individual Needs in the Primary School. London: ILEA Resources Centre.

IWANIKI, E. F. (1981). 'Contract plans; a professional ground-oriented approach to evaluating teacher performance'. In: MILLMAN, J. (Ed) Handbook of Teacher Evaluation.

JACKSON, P. W. (1979). 'The way teaching is'. In: BENNETT, N. and MCNAMARA, D. Focus on Teaching. London: Longman.

JOSEPH, SIR KEITH (1984). Speech given at North of England Education Conference, Sheffield, January.

JOSEPH, SIR KEITH (1985). Speech given at North of England Education Conference, Chester, January.

KYRIACOU, C. and NEWSON, G. (1982). 'Teacher effectiveness', Educational Review, 34, 3–12.

LUSTY, M. (1983). 'Staff appraisal in the education service', School Organisation, 3, 4, 371–378.

MCCORMICK, R. (1982). Calling Education to Account. London: Heinemann Educational.

MCKENNA, B. H. (1981). 'Context environment effects in teacher evaluation'. In: MILLMAN, J. (Ed) Handbook of Teacher Evaluation.

MCNEIL, J. D. (1981). 'Politics of teacher evaluation'. In: MILLMAN, J. (Ed) Handbook of Teacher Evaluation.

MIDWINTER, E. (1985). 'How to lose friends and not influence people', The Times Educational Supplement, 8th February.

MILLMAN, J. (Ed) (1981). Handbook of Teacher Evaluation. Beverley Hills, Calif: Sage.

MILLMAN, J. (1981). 'Student achievement as a measure of teacher competence'. In: MILLMAN, J. (Ed) Handbook of Teacher Evaluation.

MORRISON, M. and MCINTYRE, D. (1969). Teachers and Teaching. Harmondsworth: Penguin.

MORSH, J. E. and WILDER, E. W. (1954). 'Identifying the effective instructor: a review of quantitative studies, 1900–1952'. USAF Personnel Training Research Centres, Bulletin No. AFPTRC–TR–54–44.

NASH, R. (1973). Classrooms Observed. London: Routledge & Kegan Paul.

NISBET, J. (1986). 'Appraisal for improvement'. In: Appraising Appraisal. Report of a conference organized by the British Educational Research Association, March.

NORRIS, B. (1986). Report on a new Texas state examination for teachers, Times Educational Supplement, 21st March.

NUTTALL, D. (1982). Accountability and Evaluation. Course E364, Block 1. Milton Keynes: Open University Press.

PLOWDEN REPORT. GREAT BRITAIN. DEPARTMENT OF EDUCATION AND SCIENCE. CENTRAL ADVISORY COUNCIL FOR EDUCATION (ENGLAND) (1967). Children and their Primary Schools. London: HMSO.

POWELL, M. and BEARD, J. W. (1984). Teacher Effectiveness: An Annotated Bibliography and Guide to Research. New York: Garland.

RAVEN, J., JOHNSTON, J. and VARLEY, T. (1985). Opening the Primary Classroom. Edinburgh: Scottish Council for Research in Education.

ROSENSHINE, B. (1979). 'Content, time and direct instruction'. In: PETERSON, P. L. and WALBERG, H. J. Research on Teaching: Concepts, Findings and Implications. Berkeley, Calif: McCutchan.

RUSHBY, T. and RICHARDS, C. (1982). 'Staff development in primary schools: A survey of views and practice in nine schools', Educational Management and Administration, 10, 223–231.

RYANS, D. G. (1972). 'Teacher behaviour can be evaluated'. In: MOHAN, M. and HULL, R. E. Teaching Effectiveness: Its meaning, assessment and improvement. Englewood Cliffs, NJ: Ed. Tech.

SALLIS, J. (1983). 'Monitoring teacher quality', Where?, 192, October.

SALT, P. (1985). 'Heads or tails?', Times Educational Supplement, 31st May.

SCHMID, J. (1961). 'Factor analysis of the teaching complex', *Journal of Experimental Education*, 30, 1.

SHIELDS, P. (1987–88). Research for a doctoral thesis, Open University.

SMITH, B. O. (1960). 'A concept of teaching', *Teachers' College Record*, 61, 229–241.

SOCKETT, H. (1982). 'Towards a "professional" model of teacher accountability'. In: MCCORMICK, R. (Ed) *Calling Education to Account*.

SQUIRES, G. (1982). 'The analysis of teaching'. University of Hull, Newland Papers, 8.

SUFFOLK LOCAL EDUCATION AUTHORITY/DEPARTMENT OF EDUCATION AND SCIENCE (1985). *Those Having Torches. Teacher Appraisal: A Study*. Ipswich: Suffolk Education Department.

THYNE, J. M. (1963). *The Psychology of Learning and the Techniques of Teaching*. London: University of London Press.

TURNER, G. and CLIFT, P. (1985). *A First Review and Register of School and College Based Teacher Appraisal Schemes*. Milton Keynes: Open University Press.

WARWICK, D. (1983). *Staff Appraisal. Education for Industrial Society Management in Schools*. London: Education for Industrial Society.

WEAVER REPORT. GREAT BRITAIN. DEPARTMENT OF EDUCATION AND SCIENCE. (1970). *A Teaching Council for England and Wales*. London: HMSO.

WINNE, P. H. (1977). 'Aptitude treatment interactions in an experiment on teacher effectiveness', *American Educational Research Journal*, 14, 4, 389–409.

Selected bibliography and further reading

This is a very personal collection of texts which I have found most useful over a number of years in promoting thinking about all aspects of primary school teaching. Included in italics is a brief comment about each one's particular relevance. The list has to be very selective and readers will obviously have their own favourites which they are invited to add to the list. This bibliography is arranged in accordance with the six sections of the model and alphabetical order is used within each section.

Overall curriculum issues:

BRITISH BROADCASTING CORPORATION (BBC) (1985). *Multi-cultural Education: Views from the Classroom. This publication was issued in support of a video,* Anglo Saxon Attitudes, *and although not directly concerned with primary education, considers a number of issues related to schools and the promotion of anti-racist attitudes.*

DOWLING, M. and DAUNCEY, C. (1984). *Teaching 3–9 year olds: Theory into Practice.* London: Ward Lock. *For all those who teach the younger age group, this is a super book for reminding us of why we teach what, and the justification for it. Much of the theoretical underpinnings hold good throughout primary education.*

SCHOOLS COUNCIL Working Paper 75. (1983). 'Primary practice'. London: Methuen. *A good overall view of the primary curriculum, yet to be bettered in my view.*

General curriculum: learning (and playing!)

BRUNER, J. (1972). *The Relevance of Education.* London: George Allen & Unwin. *Cannot be beaten in terms of getting to the nub of educational thinking – background information of the highest level!*

CHANDLER, D. (1984). *Young Learners and the Micro-computer.* Milton Keynes: Open University. *Although a bit dated now as far as the technology is concerned, this is worth reading by those teachers who still need convincing of the various uses of the computer for teaching and learning.*

CLAXTON, G. (1984). *Live and Learn.* London: Harper & Row. *If you need to review and revise your knowledge of child (and adult) psychology, this is a very good book on background information – but don't look for many practical suggestions!*

COHEN, D. (1986). *Development of Play.* London: Croom Helm. *Another good background knowledge book with some excellent insights into children's need to play.*

DONALDSON, M. (1978). *Children's Minds.* London: Fontana. *An absolute classic, which is a thoroughly enjoyable 'read' over and over again. It contains invaluable information on the conditions for learning.*

HOLT, J. (1972). *How Children Learn* and (1973) *How Children Fail.* Harmondsworth: Penguin. *Two more 'classics', worth returning to if teachers need reminding of the processes and conditions of learning.*

JONES, R. (Ed) (1984). *Micros in the Primary Classroom.* London: Edward Arnold. *Similar comments to Chandler above but with some useful information on classroom and group organization for using the computer.*

MARKS-GREENFIELD, P. (1984). *Mind and Media,* Aylesbury: Fontana. *I have only recently come across this publication and was immediately impressed by the sensible way the author approached a whole variety of technological audio-visual aids resources and explored their potential as learning media. Very useful for the sceptics.*

It would be impossible to list books in all possible curriculum areas in the space available so I have taken a few major ones.

Specific curriculum

Language

BALL, F. (1977). *The Development of Reading Skills*. Oxford: Blackwell. *Over ten years on, this is still the best book of practical information and suggestions regarding language stimulation games, activities and resources. It also contains information on record keeping and useful lists of words.*

BLEACH, P. (1986). BBC 'Computer software for primary reading and language'. *Available from the Centre for the Teaching of Reading in Reading, this contains quite useful, up-to-date material.*

BROWNJOHN, S. (1980). *Does it have to Rhyme?* and (1982) *What Rhymes with Secret?* London: Hodder & Stoughton. *The most practical and useful books I have ever read on the subject of poetry with and for children. Most people I know who have read them have been immediately inspired to write.*

DAVIES, G. (1983). *Practical Primary Drama*. London: Heinemann Educational. *Very few books on primary drama are in evidence in libraries and none as practical as this.*

GRAVES, D. (1983). *Writing – Teachers and Children at Work*. London: Heinemann Educational. *Although other books have come along since this one, I still feel that this has the most 'meat' for those considering the needs of children when it comes to all aspects of writing.*

HUTT, E. (1986). *Teaching Language Disordered Children*. London: Edward Arnold. *An interesting book – not only for its title – which draws on many strategies for stimulatimg learning and developing a range of skills in children with specific language difficulties.*

KLEIN, G. (1985). *Reading into Racism: bias in Children's Literature and Learning Materials*. London: Routledge & Kegan Paul. *Many teachers now are giving a good deal of consideration to the quality and content of the books and resources provided for ethnically diverse schools. This book will help enormously.*

RALEIGH, M. (1981). *The Languages Book*. London: ILEA English Centre. *An excellent resource book for ideas about all aspects of verbal and non-verbal language particularly in multi-cultural contexts.*

WATERLAND, L. (1984). *Read With Me*. Stroud: Thimble Press. *The most helpful book yet to be published regarding learning to read without schemes, which covers adequately all the questions likely to be asked by teachers and others regarding progression, record keeping, skills development, etc.*

Mathematics

CHESHIRE COUNTY COUNCIL (1986 – 2nd edn). *Primary Mathematics Guidelines*. Chester. *Whether you get the first 1983 edition or the second, Cheshire can be rightly proud of these guidelines which detail, mostly through diagrams and pictorial representation, a good selection of items to be included in primary mathematics. More importantly, these guidelines make it all look fun!*

DEBOYS, M. AND PITT, E. (1980). *Lines of Development in Primary Mathematics*. Belfast: Blackstaff. *Undoubtedly the most comprehensive yet readable information ever published regarding the whole primary maths curriculum.*

DICKSON, L. BROWN M. and GIBSON, O. (1984). *Children Learning Mathematics*. Eastbourne: Holt Rinehart & Winston for Schools Council Publications. *Not only does this book give excellent practical suggestions for primary maths, but it puts it all in the framework of maths as a tool subject with underlying principles and theory. Well worthwhile for school bookshelves.*

HUGHES, M. (1986). *Children and Number*. Oxford: Blackwell. *If you have ever wondered why you or the children you teach find maths so difficult and often frustrating, this is the book for you. Although it describes research into early number learning, as the basis for consideration of children with difficulties in maths it will make good sound sense to all primary school teachers.*

Science

COUNTY OF AVON publish several Guidelines on Primary Science for both nursery, infant and junior age children. They are in flow diagram format and offer a real wealth of good ideas and suggestions for busy teachers.

WARD, A. (1986). *A Source Book for Primary Science Education*. London: Hodder & Stoughton. *A short, very readable book which begins by exploring all the key concepts within science for the five- to ten-year-olds and goes on to offer case studies and practical hints for acquiring them.*

Art

All teachers will know of the many practical books on art and craft techniques available from many sources. The following two books may be useful to help them to better understand the aesthetics underlying art teaching.

GENTLE, K. (1985). *Children and Art Teaching*. Beckenham: Croom Helm.

SUFFOLK COUNTY COUNCIL (1984). *Art 4–11: Art in the First Years of Schooling. Available from the Education Office, Suffolk County Council, Grimwade Street, Ipswich, IP4 1LJ (about £4), this is quite the most comprehensive art policy document I have ever seen. It has excellent practical suggestions as well.*

Movement

COVENTRY LOCAL EDUCATION AUTHORITY produce very comprehensive guidelines for physical education with all phases of primary education. Copies are available from Elm Bank Teachers' Centre, Mile Lane, Coventry and cost around £5 each.

Relationships with children

ALIKI (1987). *Feelings*. London: Piccolo Picture Books, Pan. *It is perhaps strange to find a children's picture book within this 'heavier' stuff. Nevertheless this has been one of my most successful resources for discussing with children their feelings about different things which happen to them in and out of school.*

BRANTHWAITE, A. and ROGERS, D. (Eds) (1985). *Children Growing Up*. Milton Keynes: Open University Press. *Again, a book concentrating on the younger end of primary but emphasizing in a wide variety of papers, why considerations at this level are so important to all stages of primary and later education.*

HOULTON, D. (1986). *Cultural Diversity in the Primary School*. London: Batsford. *An excellent philosophical and practical book for those teachers who need more information about dealing with the needs of children from culturally diverse communities.*

ROWLAND, S. (1984). *The Enquiring Classroom*. London: Falmer Press. *A very readable book with some astute observations of the interactions of children and teachers.*

TOUGH, J. (1973). *Focus on Meaning: Talking to Some Purpose with Young Children*. London: Allen & Unwin. *Still one of the few books to approach the whole question of language interaction and drawing some very pertinent conclusions.*

Children's progress and achievements

MOYLES, J. (1986). 'The whole picture', *Child Education*, 62, 3, 10–11. *The writer discusses the differences between profiling and record keeping.*

PEARSON, L. and LINDSAY, G. (1986). *Special Needs in the Primary School*. Windsor: NFER-NELSON. *This short book deals very succinctly and readably with the whole question of identification of primary age children with special needs and intervention strategies.*

It would be unfair to try to list any individual tests as being most useful because of both the diverse nature of children and the variety of possible tests. Information on NFER-NELSON's range of educational tests is available from them on request.

A good book specifically giving information about testing reading, as an example, is:

RABAN, B. (1983). *Reading – Guides to Assessment in Education*. Basingstoke: Macmillan Educational.

WHITE, D. R. and HARING, N. G. (1980). *Exceptional Children*. Columbus, Ohio: Merrill. *Since the 1981 Education Act, a great deal has been said and written about slower learners with special needs and sometimes the gifted tend to be overlooked in this category. This is a book to redress the balance.*

Discipline and child management

FONTANA, D. (1985). *Classroom Control*. London: British Psychological Society/Methuen. *A psychologists view of controlling classroom situations some of which is most practical. The rest is very useful background reading for any teacher.*

WESTMACOTT, E. V. S. and CAMERON, R. J. (1981). *Behaviour Can Change*. Basingstoke: Macmillan Educational. *This is a really lively text which guides the teacher, with cartoons, diagrams and other illustrative material, into an understanding of behaviour modification techniques for dealing with their more awkward customers.*

Classroom administration, organization and display

CROLL, P. (1986). *Systematic Classroom Observation*. London: Falmer Press. *A most helpful text for those who understand little of how to go about observing activities in the classroom. It contains useful information on different techniques for data gathering and analysis.*

MILLS, R. W. (1980). *Classroom Observation of Primary School Children – All in a Day*. London: Unwin Educational. *It is always interesting to read what someone else found out when observing classroom life.*

Teacher's professional attitudes and personality

ELLIOTT, G. (1982). 'Self-evaluation and the teacher', *Curriculum Studies*, 14, 1. *An interesting article, right to the point in terms of this book.*

LONG, R. (1986). *Developing Parental Involvement in Primary Schools*. Basingstoke: Macmillan. *A very practical and useful book for those teachers who wish to read about a wide range of ideas and activities which are helpful in order to really develop relationships with parents.*

MASHEDER, M. *Let's Cooperate*. A publication from the 1986 Peace Education Project. Available from the Peace Education Project, 6 Endsleigh Street, London WC1, approximately £2. *Rest assured 'peace' is construed in its widest terms and does not attempt to become political education. Practical suggestions for 'sociable' activities and cameos of cooperative situations are both given and the booklet also contains its own useful bibliography.*

RUNNYMEDE RESEARCH REPORT. (1985). *Education for All*. A summary of the Swann Report on the education of ethnic minority children. *Much more readable than the whole Swann Report and containing all the relevant points both for primary and secondary schooling.*

SMITH, P. (1987). *Parents and Teachers Together*. Basingstoke: UKRA/Macmillan, following the 1986 UKRA national conference. *With contributions from a wide range of people involved mostly in involving parents in children's reading, this is a source of reading pleasure as well as information.*

Appendix A: Stages in formulating the model

The original research began early in 1985 with a conviction that the development of staff within the writer's school should be the priority for the coming year. A management course had sown the seeds of an idea for staff appraisal interviews based initially on looking at the needs of the class of children and then moving on to establish the teacher's effectiveness in dealing with such needs. Then opportunities arose during the pursuit of a Master's degree to consider aspects of teacher effectiveness in greater detail.

In discussion with head and teacher colleagues within an area of the same authority, it transpired that they too were interested in exploring the construct. The research went through some five phases now very briefly outlined.

Phase 1: Information gathering

Objective – To gather as much information on effective early primary school teaching as was available and to look at the source of origins of the whole business of accountability.

Method – Details of what criteria might be used to assess teacher effectiveness and the concept of accountability were gleaned as already indicated in Chapters 1 and 2.

Outcome – A detailed list which formed the basis of the model and a wealth of research material.

Action – A variety of headings were chosen to list the characteristics of the effective primary teacher and all those gathered were then collated under the different headings.

Phase 2: Agreeing criteria

Objective – To assess how far the writer's own thinking matched that of colleagues and whether we could agree on criteria.

Method – The collated lists were distributed to teachers with some questions to promote thinking. Most schools used the documents as the basis of a series of staff meetings to discuss the construct of effective teaching.

Outcome – There was significant agreement on the contents of the document.

Action – A second document was produced and returned to schools for more comment.

Phase 3: Formulation and distribution of the first draft

Objective – To circulate a draft model and gain colleagues' further comments on content, format, sectioning, possible ways of rating or ranking the identified criteria.

Method – A revised document in a similar format to the final model was used as the basis for staff discussions again in the schools. Several teachers took individual items and assessed them for capability of giving the necessary information on teacher's performance.

Outcome – Some terminology was amended as the question of subjectivity was raised by the practical activity. The ranking scale and the histogram were incorporated as a result of recommendations from users.

Action – The model was completed in terms of format, content and presentation. The personalization element was also built in at this time.

Phase 4: Assessing suitability of use

Objective – To find out how teachers viewed the use of the model and to assess how much of a threat it might constitute to them as an appraisal document.

Method – A questionnaire was constructed and distributed which investigated teachers' responses to the document.

Outcome – Analysis of the questionnaires showed that:

1. 69 per cent felt the document had about the right number of items whilst 23 per cent thought it too lengthy. The remaining 8 per cent felt finer definitions were required.
2. 85 per cent thought the model should be used for self-evaluation, 53 per cent wanted it used as part of a whole school evaluation. 46 per cent and 36 per cent respectively wanted it used with head or senior colleagues. No one felt that school governors should have any involvement.
3. 95 per cent of all teachers felt that individual use of the model would influence them to become more effective. 78 per cent felt that a senior colleague's involvement in the model would influence them to become more effective.
4. 66 per cent wanted discussions on the results and implications of their using the model and 34 per cent thought a written report was also needed.
5. 51 per cent of respondents felt that annual appraisal would be acceptable. 49 per cent wanted termly appraisal (suggesting that the document be taken in sections to promote this).
6. 58 per cent felt the documents major advantage was that it had been prepared by and for teachers. 37 per cent felt that no real disadvantages could be highlighted, though 15 per cent of teachers thought effectiveness could not really be analysed in this way.

Action – Sufficient encouragement was gained from the information received that the document should now be used by other teachers.

Phase 5: Spreading the net

Objectives – To assess the usefulness of the model by having it piloted by teachers who had not previously been involved.

Method – A large number of teachers (teaching across the full three to eleven age range) in two other authorities were given the opportunity to comment on the model and discuss the outcome of the questionnaire analysis.

Outcome – Teachers were delighted with the model in use and confirmed the original questionnaire conclusions. A few minor additions were made to the section contents.

The model's reliability and validity

How accurately the model can be said to assess primary school teachers' effectiveness is the basis of its reliability. How far the model can actually do what is claimed for it is the essence of validity. Both were established satisfactorily by the following:

1. The model drawing heavily on the findings of previous research and primary teachers own perceptions of their role.
2. The construct as presented being quite acceptable to a range of teachers in three authorities.
3. Consistency being shown in the results of a combined self and peer/senior colleague appraisal.
4. Internal consistency being established by the writer meeting with some of the original teachers after nearly a year to undertake a kind of 'quality check'. Their attitudes to the model had remained very similar despite teacher action and the writer having changed jobs!
5. Although a subjective concept, the teachers involved agreed that face and content validity were clearly established to their satisfaction.

Appendix B: Activities to promote thinking regarding effective teaching and appraisal

Activities are suggested within broad headings which relate to aspects regarding teacher appraisal already identified in the main text. A number of key questions are raised which schools will need to consider in the near future.

Agreeing on principles of effective teaching

Activity

At a staff meeting, each member of staff is requested to write down three features she identifies as being the most important to the role of effective primary teacher. These are written large on separate sheets of paper and then pinned on an available wall. Staff then try to agree on a rank order of these items in terms of what each one sees as most important. This promotes discussion on priorities and helps to establish mutual understanding. You will probably have to agree to disagree but disagreements could well form the basis of future discussions. A similar activity could be undertaken with any particular section of the model.

Curriculum matters

Activity

A similar activity could be undertaken to that performed by the staff of a school who came up with Figure B.1 as a reminder to them of features of teaching which they should keep constantly to the fore with their class of children. Cross curricular issues could be investigated, as shown in Figure B.1 or individual curriculum areas, identified in Section 1 of the model, could be looked at systematically. This may promote new discussions on existing schemes of work and policy documents.

Teaching and learning

Activity one

As a staff, take one of your school's schemes. Try to isolate what in its contents refers directly to teaching and what to children's learning. How far is this possible? What are the consequences of attempting to do so? Many schemes concentrate directly on the

Figure B1: Cross-curricular provision for learning

Be honest. In the past half-term have all your children had the following experiences? (shade in as many areas as appropriate).

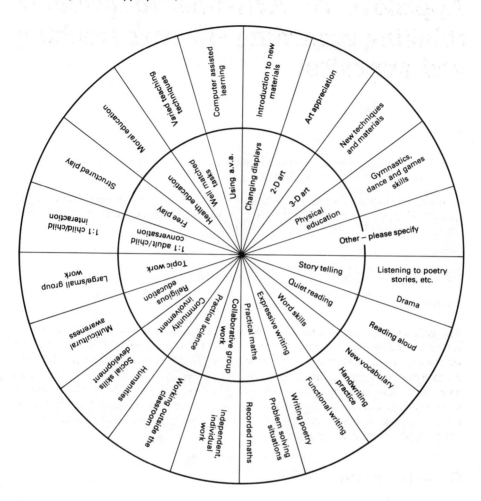

outcomes of learning and give little suggestions for teaching. How far is yours really helpful to teachers in developing effective teaching?

Activity two

Directly *teach* a group of children something appropriate to their needs on which you feel you can later test their *learning*. (Do not forget to establish first what they already know!) Ensure that some aspect of the 'test' allows children to exhibit incidental learning. Analyse what you find out about your teaching and their learning in terms of:

1 direct relationship – same words, phrases used,
   – skills acquired,
   – knowledge gained, and so on.

2 indirect relationship – ability to apply knowledge,
                             – ability to relate or transfer that knowledge to other contexts, and so on.

A good deal of research (e.g. Raven *et al.*, 1985) has suggested that learning takes place almost irrespective of teaching. How far would you agree with this? What does it mean to self-evaluation in terms of teaching and learning?

Observation of practice

Activity one

To highlight difficulties of agreement on what we actually see when making observation, get members of staff to watch a video tape (preferably a light-hearted one such as a Tom and Jerry cartoon or similar). Have prepared a set of questions which relate to setting, content, participants, methods and possibly justifications. Discuss your findings. You will hopefully learn that people see different things for different reasons.

Watch the video again and this time agree with what it is you will all look for. Some means of agreement may be reached. You should discover what are the directly observable features, i.e. who speaks to whom, when and what is said, are easy to agree upon. You will probably find that interpretation of other features, i.e. why things happened and with what outcomes, will be much more difficult to agree – even in the cartoon situation.

Activity two

Use a video of a teacher in action, either one you have made yourselves in school, borrowed from your local college or university or a commercially produced tape, i.e. the ILEA 'Monitoring Individual Needs in the Primary School' series. Analyse what each of you feels she sees in the same way as with the cartoon video. You will discover that this is very much more difficult. Factors such as what else is happening in the focus classroom distract from the actual teacher in action – a point worthy of attention if observation is to become a feature of staff appraisal determining how effective certain actions of the teacher are in developing children's learning.

Taking some action to promote change

Activity

If and when individual teachers have identified particular weaknesses in their practice, they could be allocated a sum of money from school funds to buy an 'educational' book on the topic. They would then be asked to read and make a synopsis of the book for other members of staff, reporting on the findings at a staff meeting. The writer would suggest that, in practice, it is useful if this occurs approximately half-termly, with different members of staff being involved. (The second part of the bibliography details some books which might be helpful for schools to purchase if they do not already have them.)

Self-image and self-worth

Activity

As has already been said, your perceptions of yourself must match those others have of you if self-evaluation is to be acceptable. Warning – the following activity could be painful!

Agree at a staff meeting on certain features of you all as primary teachers on which you could easily *rate* your own effectiveness and on which others could also rate you. Factors could be taken from the model but probably need to be wider, at least in the first instance. Your selection might include:

1 can speak knowledgeably about primary education;
2 relates easily to children;
3 relates well to colleagues;
4 can put a point of view clearly without being defensive;
5 has a good knowledge of resources in the school;
6 is generally supportive of and helpful to others in the school;
7 appears to really want to be effective in the job of teaching primary age children;
8 contributes well to the development of policies and practices within the school – and many more. You can decide among yourselves!

Get these printed out with a rating scale at the side of each one – a 5 to 1 scale is probably sufficient for the purpose, i.e.:

relates well to colleagues   5   4   3   2   1

Each teacher completes one herself or himself and writes his/her name on another blank form. These are then distributed randomly among the other teachers (no one need own up to whose form they complete!). This other teacher also rates a particular teacher's effectiveness on the form provided. Each teacher then compares her own rating and that of A. N. Other. If the ratings match, the teacher may well undertake a self-evaluation which would compare favourably with others' perceptions. If not, well . . . !

Appraisal involving others

Activity one: appraisal interviews

If you are trying to decide on the usefulness of such interviews to support self-evaluation or as an appraisal scheme in their own right, try the following role-play activity during a staff meeting.

Participants

You need to be in groups of three which comprise:
   – an appraiser,
   – an appraisee (being interviewed),
   – an observer.

Scenario

A colleague (senior or peer) is conducting an appraisal interview which involves discussing with the teacher how effective he or she is in the role of primary class teacher at present. Both parties are intent on conducting an efficient interview which may result in the identification of strengths and some agreed principles for future action on area(s) of least effectiveness.

The observer is to monitor the dialogue with reference to content and level of honesty and clarity in the questions, responses and statements made.

Format

(For the sake of the exercise the time must be limited. In practice, as much time as is needed should really be given.) The meeting should last no more than about eight minutes. Follow-up, with observed feedback, about five minutes. Roles within the group would, therefore, be exchanged about every 13 minutes. The process is repeated until all parties have assumed each role once.

Objectives

For teachers to: (a) assess the usefulness of appraisal interviews; (b) consider the actual needs of the parties prior to the interview taking place; (c) assess what other factors need to be considered if such interviews are to be deemed 'fair'.

You will probably discover that preparation of questions and considerations is a vital prerequisite. Self-evaluation first, *on agreed principles* (such as those identified in the model) would have made the whole process smoother, swifter and more enjoyable. It would have given the appraiser questions to ask and the appraisee the ability to talk knowledgeably and with thought on what her classroom practices are and reflect. The observer would have known a bit more about what to look and listen for!

Activity two: involving governors

It is good practice, and becoming more common in schools these days, for governors to invite members of a school's staff with particular expertise, to discuss their role within the school in terms of children's and other teachers' development. The school could nominate a member of staff to talk about the general role of the primary teacher in the same way. The model has been used by teachers in this context and proved most worthwhile and helpful to all involved. Governors have usually been amazed at the many skills required of the primary class teacher!

Activity three: considering the needs of parents

If you are, were or can speculate about being a parent, ask yourself:

> What would be the main characteristics of the ideal primary teacher for my child?
> What provision would I like to see that teacher make for my child?

If you have more than one child or can think of a relative's or friend's child whom you know, ask yourself in addition:

Would the same characteristics obtain for this child? If not, why not? Is it because the child is different, emotive feelings are not involved, the parents won't be so concerned . . . ?

Ask yourself too:

Would I recommend the school I currently teach in (a) for my own child(ren) (b) to parents of those identified 'others'? Why or why not?

And finally ask yourself really honestly (and note your answer!)

Am I the kind of primary school teacher I would wish for my own children?

Appendix C: The model for self-evaluation – assessing the effectiveness of the primary school teacher

The format of the model has been designed in such a way that, if desired, multiple copies can be made. Using the central panel on the cover as a guide, each double page spread can be photocopied on to an A4 sheet.

The model for self-evaluation

Section 1: curriculum content

I am able to provide opportunities and resources at all levels for the children's development of:

(a) Language arts (listening, speaking, reading, writing), including general vocabulary, word skills and comprehension, handwriting, drama, poetry, reading for pleasure and information, writing for different audiences and purposes and general communication skills.
(b) Mathematical concepts and skills, computation and practical use in activities related to money, shape, weight, capacity, mass, area, length, time and logic, relevant to everyday life.
(c) Scientific concepts, observational and investigative skills, encouraging children to formulate questions and hypotheses and solve problems by deduction, reasoning and testing.
(d) An awareness of the school and local environment extending to conservation and natural order as in the world at large, in the context of both past, present and future.
(e) Aesthetic awareness including interpretation, expression and skills related to music, drama, design, arts and crafts, line, form, shape, texture, colour, pattern and critical response.
(f) Social awareness and skills, living together as a school, family and local community.
(g) Physical skills and abilities, including gymnastics, small apparatus skills, creative movement and dance, games and sports and general coordination and manipulative skills.
(h) Moral and spiritual awareness and an appreciation of world beliefs and cultures and the family of man.

In curriculum aspects, I have a good knowledge and am skilled at:

i.   Story telling.

ii. Using literature to stimulate imagination and widen experiences.

iii. Using direct, first-hand experiences as a starting point for learning.

1

Personal comments:

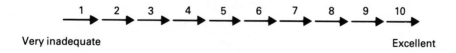

Very inadequate   Excellent

iv.   Integrating aspects of the curriculum and ensuring a sense of purpose in the tasks and activities.

v.   Encouraging the use of computers and other technological aids as learning media.

vi.   Introducing new materials/learning activities in a variety of clear and exciting ways including audio-visual aids where appropriate.

vii. Systematically organizing a sequence of skills to be acquired by children at all levels.

viii. Giving children opportunities to practise and apply new skills acquired.

ix.   Giving sufficient and interesting opportunities for reinforcement and consolidation of concepts.

x.   Providing relevant and interesting materials in all curriculum areas.

xi.   Ensuring children are taught how to use a range of equipment and undertake tasks in safety.

xii. Providing structured activities and materials to ensure progression in all curriculum areas.

xiii. Ensuring time is available for direct teaching as well as enabling and sustaining learning situations.

xiv. Providing opportunities for a variety of play situations and the use of multi-sensory approaches.

xv.   Using children's own interests to create learning situations.

xvi. Encouraging children's independence and responsibility for their own learning.

xvii. Enabling children to organize their ideas coherently and make informed judgements.

xviii. Encouraging communication and discussion between children.

xix. Recognizing children's need for a combination of seat-based and mobile activities.

xx.   Stimulating children to consider problems and reason logically on the basis of practical experiences.

xxi. Promoting children's discussion of their tasks, activities and outcomes.

Personal comments:

Very inadequate   Excellent

Section 2: relationship with children

In relating to children, I am able to:

(a) Recognize and enhance the need in every child for a positive self-image.

(b) Acknowledge and encourage children's ideas and contributions to activities.

(c) Interact with individual children every day.

(d) Thoroughly understand the personality needs of individuals and groups of children.

(e) Participate in activities alongside children.

(f) Understand when and when not to intervene in children's tasks.

(g) Communicate with children easily in verbal and non-verbal situations.

(h) Recognize the growing influence of the peer group on children's attitudes and behaviour.

(i) Be essentially positive and encouraging in all dealings with children.

(j) Provide a suitable adult 'model' for children.

(k) Make myself aware of child's background and other relevant information.

(l) Use a variety of types of questioning to elicit thoughtful responses.

(m) Make time to listen to children.

(n) Recognize the need for awareness of equal opportunities for boys and girls.

(o) Recognize the need for awareness of equal opportunities for children from all ethnic and cultural backgrounds.

Personal comments:

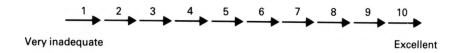

1 → 2 → 3 → 4 → 5 → 6 → 7 → 8 → 9 → 10 →

Very inadequate   Excellent

Section 3: children's progress and achievements

In attempting to ensure that each child reaches her/his full potential as far as possible, I am able to:

(a) Provide learning situations in which children succeed.

(b) Recognize and provide for the needs of the individual child.

(c) Recognize the appropriate time and type of activities to 'stretch' abler children.

(d) Recognize and provide for the needs of slower learners for activities in small steps.

(e) Keep accurate and systematic records of children's progress.

(f) Be aware of stages before and after the current teaching programme.

(g) Constantly monitor and assess the learning taking place, using testing as appropriate.

(h) Create opportunity to discuss activities, outcomes and achievements with individual children.

(i) Develop a good knowledge of learning theory and child development.

(j) Make time to observe children's attitudes and approaches to activities.

(k) Positively encourage concentration on tasks.

(l) Ensure children satisfactorily complete assignments.

(m) Keep systematic records of own planning.

(n) Use the school's schemes and policies in planning work.

(o) Prepare activities with clear aims and objectives.

(p) Present a variety of activities, though sufficient to be capable of being effectively monitored.

(q) Monitor children's abilities to transfer learning to new contexts.

(r) Organize group activities to encourage interactive learning between children.

Personal comments:

1 → 2 → 3 → 4 → 5 → 6 → 7 → 8 → 9 → 10 →

Very inadequate   Excellent

Section 4: discipline and child management

In ensuring a suitable atmosphere in which children can work and play, I am able to:

(a) Set and make known boundaries within which children can operate.

(b) Explain clearly and appropriately.

(c) Create a good atmosphere conducive to learning.

(d) Use appropriate voice level.

(e) Use praise and encouragement freely and appropriately.

(f) Use a variety of strategies for motivating children.

(g) Maintain the momentum of activities and pace appropriately.

(h) Be consistent and fair in dealing with all children.

(i) Have an awareness of the difference between a rowdy classroom and 'working' noise.

(j) Quickly recognize possible disruptive behaviour and deal with it positively.

(k) Establish a classroom routine suitable for primary school children.

(l) Encourage pupils to care for others, the school, its equipment and materials.

(m) Work with individuals or groups whilst maintaining control of the rest of the class.

(n) Show flexibility and ability to deal with more than one thing at a time.

(o) React calmly and confidently whatever the situation.

(p) Maintain high standards of behaviour expectations in the classroom and school beyond.

Personal comments:

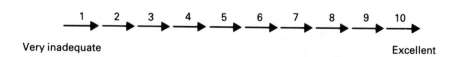

Very inadequate   Excellent

Section 5: classroom administration, organization and display

In the day-to-day running of my classroom, I am skilled at:

(a) Using combinations of whole class, group and individual teaching to maximize use of time.

(b) Organizing resources systematically.

(c) Organizing the classroom to take account of the needs of different curriculum areas.

(d) Providing a quiet area for reading or withdrawal.

(e) Encouraging children to be responsible for obtaining and returning materials.

(f) Organizing activities and materials so as to avoid timewasting queues.

(g) Ensuring familiarity with commercial materials available in the school, i.e. reading and maths schemes.

(h) Ensuring good use of the time available for children and self.

(i) Using charts, pictures, etc., to enhance learning and provide stimuli.

(j) Maintaining an interesting, exciting, orderly, attractive and thought-provoking classroom environment, inviting children's involvement.

(k) Using children's own items as the basis for learning.

(l) Creating interesting corners or tables to encourage discussion and inquiry.

(m) Displaying children's work to best advantage.

(n) Maintaining high standards of presentation of work, e.g. lettering and mounting.

(o) Monitoring the use and usefulness of various different pieces of equipment and resources.

(p) Coordinating the work of a wide range of children with different interests.

Personal comments:

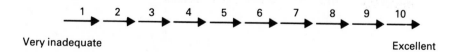

1 → 2 → 3 → 4 → 5 → 6 → 7 → 8 → 9 → 10 →

Very inadequate   Excellent

Section 6: teacher's professional attitudes and personality

In my professional status as a primary school teacher, I am:

(a) Punctual and reliable in attendance.

(b) Constantly monitoring my own performance and undertaking on-going self-evaluation.

(c) Generally enthusiastic and committed to teaching.

(d) A teacher who likes and respects children and this is reciprocated.

(e) Considered to have a warm personality and a sense of humour.

(f) Tolerant and supportive of colleagues.

(g) Professional in my approach to all school personnel and activities.

(h) Personally and professionally contributing to the 'ethos' of the school.

(i) Willing to contribute to educational and pedagogical discussions.

(j) Able to make positive relationships with the head and school staff.

(k) Able to build professional relationships with non-teaching staff, parents and community members.

(l) Helpful to those who understand less about teaching than I do.

(m) Willing to welcome the interest of parents and discuss matters of concern to them.

(n) Able to operate within large group situations with children and other staff, i.e. assembly.

(o) Willing to share ideas with others and work towards the common good of the school.

(p) Willing to take part in social and educational out-of-school activities.

(q) Willing to take advantage of INSET opportunities and keep myself up-to-date.

(r) Able to promote the use of school, LEA and DES guidelines on curriculum and other educational issues.

Personal comments:

1   2   3   4   5   6   7   8   9   10

Very inadequate   Excellent

Constraints

It is accepted that there are both environmental and administrative constraints inherent in school situations. These are identified as follows:

i. The size of the school.

ii. The number of pupils per class.

iii. The number of children in your class who have 'special needs'.

iv. The number of children from diverse ethnic and cultural backgrounds, some of whom may not have English as their first language.

v. The amount of ancillary help or assistance available on a regular basis.

vi. The level at which you are in your career, e.g. probationer, main professional grade, deputy.

vii. The level of support offered by parents and the community.

viii. The physical characteristics of the school buildings and surroundings.

ix. The school climate and ethos.

x. The materials and facilities available including financial support.

xi. The organizational structures within the school.

xii. The interrelationships within the school.

xiii. Possible curriculum constraints and mandates.

xiv. The number of non-educational tasks, i.e. money collection.

xv. The teaching time available/planned for you.

xvi. An adequate job description prepared in cooperation between you and the head/senior colleague.

Personal comments:

Histogram related to the level of effectiveness of the teacher as identified within the sections of the model

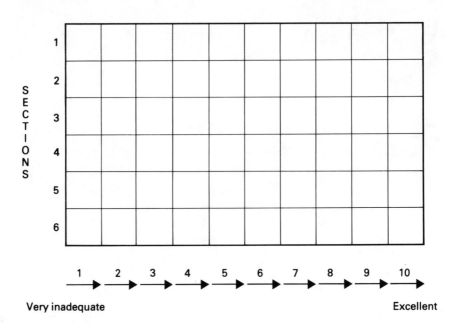